PSYCHIC
DREAMING

About the Author

Loyd Auerbach, MS (Parapsychology), is director of the Office of Paranormal Investigations (since 1989) and president of the Forever Family Foundation (since 2013), and has been in the field for more than thirty-five years focusing on parapsychological education and field investigation. Auerbach is the author or coauthor of ten books (nine on the paranormal). The most recent is *ESP Wars: East and West* (Crossroad Press, 2016), covering the psychic spying programs of the United States and the Soviet Union/Russia, which he coauthored with Dr. Edwin C. May (who ran the US program), Dr. Victor Rubel, and Joseph McMoneagle (the project's #1 remote viewer). Auerbach is a professor at Atlantic University and JFK University, and he teaches Parapsychology (local and distance) through HCH Institute in Lafayette, California, and online courses through the Rhine Education Center. He is on the Board of Directors of the Rhine Research Center and the advisory board of the Windbridge Institute. His media appearances on TV, radio, and in print number in the thousands, including ESPN's *SportsCenter*, ABC's *The View*, *Oprah*, and *Larry King Live*. He works as a parapsychologist, professional mentalist/psychic entertainer, public speaking and media/social media skills coach, and as a professional chocolatier. Visit his public speaking site at www.speakasyourself.com and his main website at www.mindreader.com.

PSYCHIC DREAMING

Dreamworking, Reincarnation, Out-of-Body Experiences & Clairvoyance

LOYD AUERBACH

Llewellyn Publications
Woodbury, Minnesota

REVISED EDITION
First Printing, 2017

This book was previously published by Warner Books in 1991 and Barnes & Noble in 1999.
Cover design: Kevin R. Brown
Cover image: Shutterstock.com/299780054/©agsandrew

Llewellyn Publications is a registered trademark of Llewellyn Worldwide Ltd.

Library of Congress Cataloging-in-Publication Data
Names: Auerbach, Loyd, author.
Title: Psychic dreaming : dreamworking, reincarnation, out-of-body experiences & clairvoyance / Loyd Auerbach.
Description: REVISED EDITION. | Woodbury : Llewellyn Worldwide, Ltd, 2017. | Includes bibliographical references.
Identifiers: LCCN 2016056364 (print) | LCCN 2017006208 (ebook) | ISBN 9780738751702 | ISBN 9780738752129 (ebook)
Subjects: LCSH: Dreams. | Visions. | Parapsychology.
Classification: LCC BF1078 .A93 2017 (print) | LCC BF1078 (ebook) | DDC 135/.3—dc23
LC record available at https://lccn.loc.gov/2016056364

Llewellyn Publications
A Division of Llewellyn Worldwide Ltd.
2143 Wooddale Drive
Woodbury, MN 55125.2989
www.llewellyn.com

Printed in the United States of America

Other Books by Loyd Auerbach

Mind Over Matter

ESP, Hauntings and Poltergeists:
A Parapsychologist's Handbook

Reincarnation, Channeling and Possession

A Paranormal Casebook

Ghost Hunting: How to Investigate the Paranormal

Hauntings & Poltergeists: A Ghost Hunter's Guide

The Ghost Detectives' Guide to Haunted San Francisco
(with Annette Martin)

ESP Wars: East and West (with Edwin C. May,
Victor Rubel, and Joseph W. McMoneagle)

Dedication

This revised edition is dedicated to my late father, Dick Auerbach. He was an inspiration and always supported my dreams, whether they came true or not.

Original Dedication: To the memories of D. Scott Rogo and Alex Tanous. As a writer, parapsychologist, and friend, Scott had an enormous influence on my professional life, my attitudes toward parapyschology, and my desire to present information to the general public. As a psychic practitioner and as a research participant at the ASPR, Alex, too, had an impact on my professional base. More, though, he somehow led me to experience what people call "psychic." You will both be missed.

Contents

Acknowledgments

For this new revision: A big thank you goes out to Annie Wilder, for reaching out to me and arranging for the reincarnation of *Psychic Dreaming*, and to all my students who have allowed me into their lives over the years.

Back in 1991, with the original edition of *Psychic Dreaming*, I acknowledged the following—I've added a couple of comments here.

In writing my first book (*ESP, Hauntings and Poltergeists*) I thanked everybody who had a hand in the making of me, personally, in the field of parapsychology. You are all thanked again.

As for this volume, I'd like to especially thank several people I interviewed, including Keith Harary, Beth Hedva, Montague Ullman (since passed away), Joanne Mied, and Pat Kampmeier, for giving me time and putting up with my questions.

Thanks to Kathy Dalton, Doug Day, and Brian McRae, for moral support, and to Rachel Seaborn, for helping Kathy and Doug go through a lot of letters.

A special nod of the head to my agent for this book (the 1991 and 1999 editions), Linda Mead, to Brian Thomsen who came up with the idea for this book, and to Beth Lieberman, for being a great editor to work with (again, for the 1991 edition).

Thanks again to the great people I worked with at LexisNexis (formerly Mead Data Central) in San Francisco. It was great being there, and without the LexisNexis information services I'd have had a much tougher time writing the proposal (let alone the book).

Special thanks go to Marcello Truzzi, for keeping me abreast of a lot of happenings in and around parapsychology (and for all the jokes). Marcello passed away several years ago and is sorely missed.

Lots of love to my parents, Barbara and Dick Auerbach, and to my brothers, Ron and David, for their continued support. My father passed away a little over ten years ago, though I still feel his presence in my life.

Preface

When I first published *Psychic Dreaming* in 1991, it was one of three books subtitled "A Parapsychologist's Handbook" (the other two being *ESP, Hauntings and Poltergeists* in 1986 and *Reincarnation, Channeling and Possession* in 1993). All three included extensive background on the history of parapsychology and the state of research at the time, as well as appendices that took readers to a variety of other parapsychological resources. They were intended to be something different from the book you now hold in your hands (or on your eReader).

I was asked to revise *Psychic Dreaming* to focus on how dreams and psi work together, and how you, the reader, can work with your own dreams, psychic or otherwise. Given the new focus, much of the parapsychological background has been removed during the revision process. As the scope of the project was really to reprint the most relevant material (in a more flowing form) from the original, there has been only minor updating—mostly pop cultural and in reference to technology (after all, no one really uses a VCR anymore).

Even though the latest research on sleep and dreaming has not been included in this book, the process of working with dreams has not changed. Nor have there been any appreciable new findings on psychic dreams from parapsychology (perhaps mainly due to the lack of research funding in general for the field).

Consequently, the material is still robust and relevant enough that this revised reprint will get you well on your way examining, understanding, and working with your dreams in general, and your psychic dreams in particular.

Introduction

One of the more frequent questions a parapsychologist (and certainly a psychologist) gets asked outside of their regular working situations is "I had this dream ... can you tell me what it means?" Of course, the psychic twist to all this is the second question of "Will it come true?"

Many people are fascinated by experiences we call psychic, but more people, including skeptics of the psychic, are even more infatuated with the surreal (though often frighteningly real) world of our dreams. We want to know why we dream certain things, what they mean, how we can control them, and if they will come true (or have they already happened). There are dozens of books available on dreams, everything from interpretation books to workbooks to books with particular scientific emphases, from psychology to neuropsychiatry. There are many books on the paranormal that touch on dreams, even a few that deal specifically with dreams and their connection to a particular psychic ability, such as telepathy. But I wanted to write a book that examines the potential range of psychic components of our dreams, with the idea of offering suggestions on how to use that information.

In this book, I will explore both sides of the ESP/dream connection. To understand how psychic information can appear in dreams, in what form and through what sort of interpretations, we need to look at dreams, sleep, and the dreaming process in the brain. To understand the forms of psychic abilities and information and how such can be used by those of us who have such experiences through our dreams, we need to look specifically at the different kinds of experiences, at least in the ways they are categorized by parapsychologists today. In order to understand how to work with information that may come through our dreams, we need to look at the connection between those experiences and the form and process of dreams.

Some of you reading this book after most of my others may seem a bit surprised that it is dealing with dreams. After all, from most of my writing and media exposure, you have come to believe that Loyd Auerbach is a "ghostbuster" and nothing more. In actuality, parapsychology covers so much more than mere things that go bump in the night, and I have always considered myself more of a generalist in the field, with some obvious emphasis on survival of bodily death and all that includes. But one really can't effectively study ghosts and hauntings and the like without understanding other psychic experiences and what parapsychologists have learned in the laboratory as well as during their field investigations.

Much of my focus has been as someone who reaches out to the public with the intent of showing how common psychic experiences are. I've done that through the media, through my writing in print and on the web, and through the many courses I've taught for adults (and on occasion, people younger than that) academically and non-academically. My professional background started right after graduating with a master's degree in parapsychology in the early 1980s with a position in Public Information and Education at the American Society for Psychical Research. Over the years, I've been heavily involved in teaching parapsychology, doing field research and investigation, working with and within various organizations, writing, and even a bit of laboratory research (though mainly as a consultant looking at potential fraud and the controls for the experiments).

One of the things I've always prided myself on has been awareness of the work of others in and around my field. This book would not have been possible without the work of others, allowing me much to synthesize as I put it through my own mental processing.

The idea for a book on dreams and their psychic component was actually not my own. The idea for this book came straight from the editor of my first book, Brian Thomsen (then with Warner Books). When it was suggested to me, I got excited about it (why hadn't I dreamed of it?). As I started looking further into my field's research on the subject, my curiosity was truly aroused—the result being the first version of *Psychic Dreaming*, first published in 1991.

It's been revised (though not necessarily updated, other than minor bits) for the current audience with more of a focus to help you better understand how psychic information passes into and out of dreams, how to identify it, and how to work with your dreams so as to be able to potentially use that information.

Dream along with me...

chapter 1
Psychic Means What?

The title of this book is *Psychic Dreaming*. While a good deal of the first part of this book deals with sleep and dreaming, it's important to set the foundation for the psychic aspect: What does it mean to be psychic or to have psychic experiences?

Parapsychology, Psi, and Psychic

Parapsychology is the scientific study of psychic, or psi (pronounced sigh), phenomena. These are exchanges of information between living things (mainly people, of course), between the minds of living things and the environment (without the use of what we call our normal senses), or are direct influences of the minds of living things on the environment (without the use of physical bodies or technology). Of course, these interactions do not seem to be currently explainable by the known physical laws of nature, but that will not always be the case. *Psi*, by the way, is the term chosen by parapsychologists to refer to these experiences because it is a fairly clean term, being the twenty-third letter of the Greek alphabet and denoting simply an unknown.

To say you are *psychic* may simply mean that you have some other way besides logical deduction or inference to come up with information to solve problems. Whatever it is we're using to gain extra insight, whether we use jargon terms like *psi* or *ESP* or not, is something worth paying attention to; our minds are telling us, "There's a bit of information that needs considering... so consider it already!"

People who call themselves psychic can run a wide range, since everyone has some degree of psychic ability, according to the tenets of parapsychology. However, there are those who call themselves psychic with a capital P. "I am a Psychic" is a different phrase than "I am psychic." So, the people claiming to be *a Psychic* are people who have, by their own statements, a better grasp of their own abilities, and therefore some degree of control of those abilities. Such a job title (psychic or psychic reader or psychic practitioner) often doesn't mean that person really has any degree of actual control of their abilities, but only that they recognize all the extra information coming into their minds, and that they can utilize or apply that information in different situations. And, of course, there are many phonies out there—people who not only are not terribly psychic (not any more than anyone who visits them as clients) but are also aware of their unpsychicness and fraudulently put themselves out there as "ones who know."

Being Psychic

In looking at whether some people are more psychic than others, we have to define terms. Someone who is *psychic* is someone who has psychic abilities and experiences. Since the majority of human beings have experienced something psychic in their lives, and since the experiments in parapsychology indicate that psi is evenly distributed across the population, as are the reports of psychic experiences, it would appear that *everyone is psychic to some degree.* Whether one person is more psychic than another is a valid question, but one difficult to assess in a given case.

The analogy used to relate psi to something in science fiction is that psi is like musical talent. Everyone has it to some degree, whether that means you can tap your foot to a beat or can play a concerto on a piano. Recognition of musical talent is a key to developing it. Some people are child prodigies, able to jump right into the music with little or no training, and others, try as they might throughout their lives, can never get any better than playing "Chopsticks."

Psi is similar, though certainly not as trainable. Being psychic may mean recognizing the difference between information received or perceived by your normal senses and anything extra that comes through. It may be that those people who call themselves psychics are able to separate that noise they get through their senses and pick up fainter signals from the background.

According to all polls, most people in the West do believe psychic interactions and experiences are at least possible, even if our culture (especially academia) says otherwise and even makes fun of the belief. In a poll conducted in the latter part of the 1980s by George Gallup Jr. and Jim Castelli, and reported in the *Los Angeles Times* (Dick Roraback, "If There's a Ghost of a Chance, Americans Will Believe It," October 31, 1988), 46 percent of all Americans believe in extrasensory perception, 24 percent believe in the ability to receive information from the future (precognition), and 15 percent believe in ghosts.

In a similar poll conducted by the University of Chicago's National Opinion Research Center and reported by priest/novelist Andrew Greeley, 42 percent of Americans report contact with someone who died, and 67 percent believe in ESP. Surveys and polls of groups around the country have reported similar numbers. So a hefty percentage of people believe in psychic experiences and have reported them. With such high numbers of experients, the image often projected by opponents to parapsychology and by many psychic practitioners that these experiences are not normal is false. Psychic experiences, or those we call psychic, are in actuality part of the normal range of human experience.

More recent polls show that college-educated people are more likely to believe in psi's reality or at least possible existence, with upward of seven out of ten people believing in some form of psychic experience.

Millions of people have reported experiences they have classified as psychic or paranormal. Parapsychologists study those experiences and try to isolate what we think may be causing them. We are also looking for the physical explanations for how psi might work, how people might gain information from the future or the past or from thousands of miles away, or how we might possibly be able to affect that computer across the room. We study the how (psi happens), who (it happens to), and why (it happens to those people).

Parapsychologists study subjective paranormal experiences (SPE). This phrase, coined by neuropsychiatrist and parapsychological researcher Dr. Vernon Neppe, describes very well what happens to people. The SPE relates to any experience one has that seems or feels paranormal or psychic. We call it subjective because it is that personal interpretation that the experience is out of the normal range of experience and can be called psychic. This does not mean the SPE doesn't relate to objective, real happenings, just that the objective, real evidence might not be available.

What Falls Under the Psi Label?

Extrasensory perception (ESP) is the interaction involving information flowing into someone's mind. For physical interactions—the idea of mind over matter—parapsychologists use the term *psychokinesis (PK)*, covering everything from psychic healing to affecting computers and other electronics to movement of objects.

Parapsychologists study these phenomena both in and out of the laboratory, as these things happen spontaneously in people's lives. Parapsychologists apply the scientific method to study psychic experiences, and this involves much more than just collecting stories from people. In addition, the idea that the human personality, spirit, soul, or mind can survive the death of the body has also involved parapsychologists from the very start, and is its own subcategory of psi phenomena, called *Survival of Bodily Death.*

ESP

To further drill down in the categories, ESP is basically receptive in nature, as our minds receive information from other sources. When the information apparently has its start or origin in the mind of another person (or even an animal) we call it *telepathy*, mind-to-mind communication. Unlike what you see on television, this really doesn't mean that someone can read another person's mind. It's more the idea that images, sensations, and information can somehow be shared between two or more minds directly. As far as dreams are concerned, we are looking at the idea that in our dreams information that originates in the minds or experience of others somehow finds its way into our dreams, sometimes leading to mutual or shared dreaming.

Clairvoyance is an idea that goes way back in human history. This is the ability to visually perceive objects, people, or events happening at the same moment as vision but outside the range of our ordinary senses or inference. Most people have visions or essentially see the information in their mind's eye apparently because sight is the sense we rely on the most. When the psychic information comes into our heads, our brains translate it into imagery as the first form of perception. *Clairvoyance* means "clear seeing," but people also relate mentally hearing psychic information (*clairaudience* means "clear hearing," with the mind's ear). In addition, we often bodily feel or sense things happening elsewhere (clairsentience) and there are reports of smelling things at a distance (clairscent or clairaliance). Parapsychologists simply use clairvoyance as a catch-all for the variations.

While we're not quite sure just what determines whether someone will receive psychic information visually, or through hearing, feeling, smelling, or even tasting, it may actually relate to what kind of person you are. Are you primarily visual, auditory, or kinesthetic (feeling with your body)? This may affect just what form psychic information takes in your perception, and of course, in your dreams.

Another term used in more recent decades for such real-time psychic perceptions is *remote viewing,* or, more properly, *remote perception.* These phrases have been well-used since the early 1970s, and they more correctly identify the ability we're often looking at—we perceive things, people, or events from a remote location. Experiments in remote viewing have provided a good base of information supporting the existence of psi of this type, and the results of the US government's program (1972–1995, called Star Gate for the second half of its existence) provide excellent examples of this (see the 2016 book I coauthored with Edwin C. May, Victor Rubel, and Joseph McMoneagle, *ESP Wars: East and West*).

But while telepathy and clairvoyance relate to things happening at the same moment as when the person receives the information, most of us think of psychic visions as relating to the future (or, at least that's what the tabloids and the skeptics would have us believe).

The apparent ability to receive information from future events is called *precognition*. Clairvoyance crosses space to grab information, while precognition crosses both space and time. In other words, one doesn't only seem to get information about your own location in the future, but also about events and locations far away from where you are now or even will be in the future.

We do have problems separating telepathy and clairvoyance in many situations. For example, let's say our experiment involves you going to a distant place, and at that time I am to describe that location. Let's say I am able to give a rather good description of that place. The question is, am I describing the location by psychically tuning in on *it* or am I tuning in on *your mind,* relating what you are observing or what you are looking at.

In a psychic dream, we have the same problem. If the dream I have relates to something happening to you at that moment, am I receiving the information from your mind or am I somehow describing the situation, the place, or the events by psychically observing it directly? *Does it really matter which?* Probably not. It is still happening somehow. We call that psi.

To further complicate things, precognition has more recently come into play as the possible explanation for much of what we thought of as real-time psi. For the remote viewing example, could I be precognitively picking up on the feedback I will get once the experiment is over, shown photos of the actual target, or even taken there after my guesswork?

As you might imagine by these examples, it's difficult to create a true telepathy experiment, since if someone observes the target the information could come from either the mind of the observer or from the target itself, at the moment of the guesswork or from future feedback. In either case, psi is operating, and that's what is most important, at least for the time being.

It's easier to create a clairvoyance experiment, since all we need do is have the target, whether a photo, drawing, card, symbol, coordinates of a distant location, or other information source sealed up in an envelope or maybe flashed on a video monitor in a sealed room with no one there to see it. To be a decent experiment, the target must be randomly selected from many other sealed targets (or maybe randomly selected by a computer programmed with a number of locations), so that no one could possibly know what the target is. With no one observing the target, the possibility of telepathy has been ruled out.

Predicting the Future

We constantly hear of people making predictions of future happenings (just look at the tabloids at the beginning of each year…"Top Ten Psychics Predict…"), and, as the skeptics have pointed out, we hardly ever hear of the outcome of those predictions if they've failed. Psychics often state after the event has occurred that "I predicted it months ago." Rarely can they produce evidence that supports that claim.

Psychics also often relate general predictions to events as they occur, such as "a major world leader will die next year" or "a disaster will occur sometime in the next few months claiming many lives." I can predict, especially right now, writing this particular chapter in October 1990, a year after the San Francisco Bay Area earthquake of 1989, that there will be several earthquakes of 3.0 and above before the end of 1991 (or 1992, etc.) in northern California. Those of us living in the aftermath of the 7.1 quake in northern California have already experienced many aftershocks of that quake measuring 3.0 and greater. And, unfortunately, there are bound to be more.

But there are hundreds of reports of specific incidents predicted and coming true, not months in advance but often hours or minutes. Such premonitions are not generally about earth-shattering (or quaking) events. Rather they are more personal. These may be sensations that you may be in danger if you do something tomorrow, like get on a particular ship or plane that turns out to be at the center of an accident, or maybe that you will run into a friend you haven't seen in years this afternoon (and you do), or perhaps that a relative or a friend may die suddenly (not of a lingering illness... that could be guesswork) or that a friend or a relative is offered a new job or wins the lottery.

Most predicted events that come true (or don't come true) involve human decision-making (should I take that flight or not ...should I bet on that horse or not?). In studies of precognitive experiences, it's been related that the overwhelming number of experiences involve predictions where outcomes would be different if a different decision was made.

In dreams, precognized events seem to be more easily remembered, but they can also be confused with other dream imagery.

How do you know it's a precognition of the future or simply our wishful thinking in our dreams? You can't always, until the event happens. And sometimes, you can't even remember that you had the dream until the events start occurring.

If you have ever been in a situation where you suddenly feel as though you'd experienced it before, you may know that sensation is called déjà vu. Defined as the feeling that you've "seen this before," Dr. Vernon Neppe has identified close to fifty possible explanations for the déjà vu experience where all but a few are psychic explanations (others range from associating incorrect memories of a similar situation to actually having been in that place before).

One of those psychic explanations is that the sense of familiarity results from your having had a precognitive dream of the situation, a dream you possibly forgot. As you get into the situation, the memory of the dream comes flooding back into your mind, giving that déjà vu sensation, and with it sometimes the full memory of the dream that tells you what's going to happen next. Sound familiar? I've had a number of those experiences and have spoken with many people who have had them as well.

Of course, that's all to say that there is a way to actually receive information from the future, or that the future even exists for us to gain information from. This in itself is a problem, since we have theories and models of how time works, but we really don't know for sure. I'll discuss this more as we get to the chapter on precognitive dreams. At this point, suffice it to say that it seems that the future is always in motion, to paraphrase a certain Jedi Master named Yoda. No one knows this better than the meteorologists trying to predict the weather.

If we do acknowledge that it's somehow possible to gain information from the future (which may or may not yet exist), then it follows, perhaps more easily, that we can somehow gain information from the past (which has already happened). We call the ability when information comes psychically from past events *retrocognition*. In other words, information comes from some past object, event, or person without the use of normal senses or logical inference or through looking up the records. Such peering into the past does seem to occur in the dream state and may even be related to reincarnation.

Out-of-Body Experiences

When one draws a connection between dreaming and psychic experience, there are two types of such experiences that immediately come to mind. One is the precognitive dream. The other is out-of-body experiences (OBEs). If that language doesn't sound familiar, consider the occultists' term *astral projection*. The idea of OBEs is not strictly psychic in nature as defined by parapsychologists or psychologists, it is simply the experience or feeling or sensation that you are somehow outside of your own body. The concept of astral projection is that somehow the spirit or soul (or astral body) leaves the physical shell of the body for a time. Since there is nearly no scientific evidence available that there is an astral form that can truly leave the body behind, let's stick with the OBE definition.

Strictly speaking, an OBE is a psychological one, not necessarily psychic. Have you ever had the experience or dream that you were floating outside your body and possibly were even able to look down on it? That could be dream imagery or just the mind giving you some imagery that fits what you're feeling at that time.

Have you ever felt that while out of your body you traveled some-place else? If that happened while you were dreaming, maybe it was just that: a dream that you left your body behind and flew away. If it happened while awake though relaxed (which is the state that OBEs most often occur), again it could have been something analogous to a daydream. This is psychological, but not necessarily psychic.

But let's say in your travels you overheard a conversation in another part of your house or apartment building. Or maybe you observed something happening in another country, where you traveled while out of body. And let's say that the observations checked out, that the conversation really occurred or the event in that other country did happen. That perception of events outside the range available to your physical body just made your psychological OBE a psychic one.

Doesn't that sound similar to a remote viewing, the only difference being that you somehow traveled to the distant location rather than simply picking up information? Yes, it is similar, and the reason may be that they are the same experience. Whether it's clairvoyance rather than the idea of part of your consciousness (or all of it) will be discussed later.

Surviving Death: Apparitions

Psychical researchers in the nineteenth century used the term *Survival of Bodily Death* to refer to the concept that some part (or all) of human consciousness survives the death of the physical body and somehow retains its intelligence (and generally its personality). The main concepts here relate to this Survival, and some absolutely intrude into our dreaming.

The most obvious would be apparitions, or what most people generally call ghosts. An apparition is what is seen, heard, felt, or smelled and is related to some part of the human personality/ mind/soul that can somehow exist in our physical universe after the death of its body. The basic idea of an apparition is twofold: the consciousness must survive and it must be able to communicate or otherwise interact with people.

When I say that the apparition is seen or heard, I don't mean that this is happening through the eyes or ears. Remember that our actual perception of the world around us involves a process whereby data is received by the senses, then screened and enhanced by the brain and mind. Perception resides not in the senses, but in the brain. Hallucinations, for example, are essentially superimposed images, sounds, smells, etc. that are added to (or in other instances blocked or erased from) the information of our senses. Dreams have highly visual and auditory content that is clearly from within our minds.

In the same way, the apparition somehow adds information to our sensory input that is then processed with our sensory data and integrated in what we perceive. In other words, the mind of the ghost is providing our own minds with the extra information necessary to perceive him or her.

Apparitions have been known to intrude on or communicate with the living in their dreams. Apparitions are often confused with hauntings, often referred to as "residual hauntings" by ghost hunters. Hauntings are place or object centered and the activity is repetitive and does not react to the living. So the difference is that apparitions are essentially "live" (conscious beings) and hauntings are "recordings." We (living people) pick up on information somehow encoded into the environment, either clairvoyantly or through some connection between the brain and the physical environment, possibly the geomagnetic field.

Interestingly enough, many apparitions sighted are of living people. Those people may be in some kind of crisis or distress, though often there can be a correlation to a time when they are dreaming (generally dreaming of visiting the place they're seen) or even having an OBE.

Near-Death Experiences (NDE)

An experience that strongly suggests Survival of Bodily Death is the near-death experience (NDE). While there are many people who effectively die (heart stops, possible extreme lowering of brain activity) who have no recollection of any kind of experience, we know the NDE as one in which there is some kind of conscious experience during that period—an experience that for some percentage of people has some psychic earmarks and leads to fundamental shifts in their outlook on life and death. One characteristic of the NDE is an OBE, the individual recalling leaving his or her body, sometimes observing the location and people around the near-dead body. In some reports, the individual goes farther afield and can report back on events and people well outside the sensory range of the body. This is the psychic/ESP component of the NDE.

In most Western NDEs, the experient will see a tunnel of some sort with a light at the end of it, while in some reported Asian NDEs there's a bridge over a river or a stream and a garden of some sort. Once through the tunnel or across the bridge, they may meet with a familiar figure, typically a deceased family member or friend or a religious figure. The experient may be told it is not yet his or her time or personally decides that it is not yet time to die.

In any event, the body is resuscitated, and the person finds himself or herself back in the body, with a recollection of what happened.

The only real connection to dreams seems to be that the experients may initially think they are dreaming during the actual NDE, and of course, the skeptics have claimed this is all a mental construct like a dream.

Reincarnation

Reincarnation, the ancient idea of the spirit or soul reborn in another body, is accepted in some form or another by a number of the world's many religions and believed by well over a billion people on the planet today. Parapsychologists are very careful when looking at supposed cases of reincarnation, and they usually stay away from hypnotic regression as a means to produce information on past lives, for reasons you'll see later in the book. For us, the cases most suggestive of reincarnation are those involving very young children. Having developed neither a strong individual personality nor a vast amount of memories (especially of past events), children who remember past lives spontaneously, without any prompting from a hypnotist, are intriguing case studies. These cases have implications for our understanding of consciousness, whether one comes at the explanation from a psychic, mystical, religious, neurobiological, or purely skeptical perspective.

A Little on PK

As mentioned earlier, parapsychologists also study psychokinesis (PK). Very few dreams seem to be connected to psychokinetic experience, although having some understanding of dreams and their imagery can help us look at and decipher the meaning of psychokinetic experiences as they occur in everyday life. In addition, some parapsychologists consider any impact of the mind on one's own body to be a form of PK, whether from the conscious or unconscious/dreaming mind.

So in looking at the phenomena in a given poltergeist case, we have the analogy to dreamwork. We look for what the specific effects may represent or relate to in the experience/life of the "agent" (or dreamer, if we were working with a dream). Working through the issue resolves the problem/frustration/stress that brings up the recurrent spontaneous psychokinesis (RSPK) to begin with. The recurrence of the PK halts, as a recurrent dream might stop after identifying and working through the issue at the root of that repeating dream.

There is also the consideration that what we dream might cause some ripples in the world outside of ourselves. That the unconscious can in some rare cases have a PK impact on the physical world directly is clear from poltergeist cases. In such cases, a living person (not a spirit) is at the center of what is typically chaotic, unexplained activity, from movement and breakage of objects to unusual behavior and crashes of electronics. In 1958, William G. Roll, working from an earlier foundation of work by Nandor Fodor, formed a model of RSPK: the unconscious of a typically stressed (emotional/psychological) individual essentially relieves that stress outward in the world with PK in an uncontrolled, spontaneous fashion.

Often the actual activity can be looked at the same way one might work with dream imagery. Is what moves/happens related to issues in the poltergeist agent's life? This is the greatest connection between dreaming (actually dreamwork) and PK.

However, that's not to say it's impossible for someone to psychokinetically affect things around them while dreaming. It's just a bit more difficult to judge, as the occurrences don't form the same kinds of patterns as in poltergeist cases.

In pop culture, this dreams-affect-reality theme is more evident, though usually in a big way. In the classic science fiction novel by Ursula K. Leguin *The Lathe of Heaven*, made into a TV movie in the 1980s and more recently a TV miniseries, a man has the ultimate PK ability attached to his dreams. Any changes in the world he dreams of have come true when he wakes up. Unfortunately, so complete are the changes that all people (except himself) have had their memories altered, so no one except the dreamer even remembers the world as it was before the change.

In the classic horror film series *A Nightmare on Elm Street*, Freddy Krueger is alive only in the shared dreamworld of humanity and appears capable of selecting the dreams of particular victims, pulling often more than one person into a shared dream, then manipulating that world with dire effects for the person being attacked in the dream. In that series, the person killed in a dream doesn't merely die quietly, but rather there seems to be a psychokinetic effect on the victim's body, with people slashed in a dream slashed in reality, and so forth.

Well, if any of that was going on, we may never really know. There doesn't appear to be any way, outside of literary license, to invade the dreams of another. And while there is a good deal of folklore around about the effects of dreaming something bad having a correlation in real life, the facts don't really fit. One such tale I often hear is "If you are falling in a dream and don't wake up before you hit the ground, you'll die." That doesn't fit, especially since people do have dreams of falling and do sometimes dream of hitting the ground. (In their dreams, they can usually get up, brush themselves off, and continue with the dream, kind of like Wile E. Coyote.) It certainly doesn't fit with the number of dreams reported where the dreamer finds him or herself in the midst of an accident or disaster, seeing themselves die, or getting otherwise hurt. No real effect, other than perhaps a psychological one. Unfortunately, if people do die this way, we'd probably not know it at all, that is, unless the person hung around as an apparition.

Belief Is Important to Psi

Past studies in parapsychology have linked belief to lab experiments. Since the 1950s, the Sheep-Goat Effect, first described by Gertrude Schmeidler, has shown again and again that believers in psi tend to score above chance in experiments, while disbelievers tended to score below chance. This makes good sense in light of performance psychology. People do better when they believe they can do what they're trying to do. As with athletes and their sports or with students taking tests, belief in their own skill or in success is important. It would appear that human beings must, in general, have some belief that they can complete a task, that the task is possible, for any success at all. Doubt in our ability is often our undoing in everyday tasks, and that seems to be so where psi is concerned as well. Going forward, remember this, as believing you can increase your recollection and even affect your own dreams is a key element to doing so.

Laboratory Psi Research That Connects to Dreams

Most research on psychic dreams, or any occurrence of psi in dreams, is done through examination of the actual content of people's reported dreams and seeing if that connects with events, people, and locations the dreamer was unaware of. Some research has been done under laboratory conditions, mostly focused on dream telepathy. I'll be discussing this particular parapsychological research in chapter 8.

One other line of research relates somewhat to our topic of dreams. The dream state is an altered state of consciousness (ASC). Work with such altered states has involved everything from hypnosis to biofeedback. Research called ganzfeld experiments—much of it originally conducted by the (no longer in operation) Psychophysical Research laboratories in Princeton, New Jersey, in the 1980s and by numerous researchers around the world since then—has yielded extremely good and generally repeatable results.

The ganzfeld, or "whole field," setting involves a person designated as a receiver who is placed in mild sensory deprivation. The person reclines on a comfortable couch and has sight cut off through the use of halved ping-pong balls placed on the eyes and hearing cut off through headphones that play only white noise, or static. In another room, the sender, usually a friend or a relative, is looking at a video monitor. Once the experimenter starts things up, it's all run by computer, the experimenter knowing nothing of the target selection until after the experiment has run its course.

The computer randomly selects a video clip from hundreds, then presents that clip on a monitor for the sender several times, while the receiver says anything that comes to mind of what is being perceived, as in a daydream. This is recorded by the experimenter over a microphone system. When the video runs its course, the experimenter reads back what the receiver described. The receiver is asked to remove the headphones and blinders and is shown four video clips chosen by the computer, one of which is the actual target. He/she tries to rate each one, giving (hopefully) the highest ranking to the actual target.

Finally, the actual target is revealed by the computer to both receiver and experimenter. The experimenter checks both the ranking and the descriptions against the actual targets, and the descriptions and all four video clips are sent out to independent judges to do their own rankings and matching of descriptions to any/all of the targets.

Scoring in the ganzfeld setting has been as high as 50 percent, though more consistently in a range of 38 percent, much higher than chance. In an examination and subsequent debate on the ganzfeld experiments by experimenter Charles Honorton and critic Ray Hyman, there was some agreement. There was, as both concluded, "something" happening out of the ordinary, a communications anomaly worthy of further study, but while Honorton suggested psi as responsible for that "something," Hyman couldn't agree to that interpretation.

ESP in Children

I'm often asked if children are more psychic than adults, if we lose our abilities as we grow up. It would seem that children appear to be more psychic only through a twist of fate, that being education. Children don't question or categorize their experiences in the same way adults do; they haven't always learned that things like "knowing what's in Uncle Harry's mind" or "making that ashtray move by itself" are impossible. We seem to be educated out of being psychic as we grow up, learning to question and even disregard experiences that don't fit the norm. This is quite evident when you look at cultures whose belief systems incorporate psychic happenings, and when you look at the previously mentioned Sheep-Goat

Effect. Bring in doubt and disbelief and you drop scoring and ignore the experiences.

Of course, we also can't rule out the power of a child's imagination in a given situation. It is not responsible to view every report from a child as psychic just because it fits under that category. In looking at any psychic experience after the fact, whether ours or someone else's, it is necessary to look at all possible explanations and to discard the normal possibilities first before assuming something is paranormal.

How Does Psi Work?

What about explanations for how psi works? That is problematic in itself, as we may be trying to explain something without the words or physics to do it justice. Discovering electricity is a far cry from understanding what it is and how it works. There are many theories and models of psychic functioning, how it is possible to relay data without the use of the normal senses, or how it is possible to affect matter directly with our minds. As we proceed with the study of dreams and connection with psychic functioning, I'll try to address some of those concepts.

What can parapychologists do with dreams? As you move through this book, you will discover the answer to that question. As mentioned, there has been much research in the area of telepathy in dreams and recent discussion of how Earth's magnetic field affects the incidence of telepathy, clairvoyance, and precognition in dreams (and in the waking state). As we work with our own dreams, we may learn not only to control the content of the dream, but also to ask for specific information to come into that dream—information that may be beyond our own memory and experience and senses (and therefore psychic). Parapsychologists looking for experiences to research or explain and study can use dreams as source material for psychic experience. Since we all dream every night, and since it would appear that many people (if not everyone) can learn to recall and even affect the content of their dreams, such a form of human experience may be a fertile ground in which to plant the suggestion to have a psychic experience.

Are *you* psychic? If our research, both in and outside of the laboratory is any indication, yes, you've probably had at least one experience that could be classified as psychic, one that you may have a name or label for now that you've learned the kinds of experiences and abilities parapsychologists deal with. But remember, words can be deceiving. The words I've used to describe psychic abilities, even the word *psychic* itself, may be inadequate to describe what's really going on here, or may be inaccurately describing something else entirely.

And where dreams are concerned, it seems that anything is possible.

chapter 2
In Your Dreams

I woke up this morning, groggy as usual, partially remembering something or other. I knew I had dreamed something, but I couldn't quite get it. My alarm had gone off when I was in the wrong stage of sleep, for me anyway, at a point where my brain just couldn't quite even pull together anything more than just a suggestion of what the dream had been about.

So what good are dreams if we can't remember them? When we train ourselves to remember them, as many people have, are they worth anything to our conscious minds and daily lives? Those dream analysis books tell us lots of things about the value of dreams and what just about each and every item or object or event means, even if the books differ from author to author. Are dreams always merely symbolic—pieces of experience that we must analyze to get anything out of them—or can they simply give us the plain truth from time to time, taken at face value?

Dreams seem to be mostly extensions of our own experience, although, as I hope to show you in this book, there is a possibility that they're more than that. Dreams may be a perfect vehicle for information to flow from both our creative sides and from the outside world through psychic ability, although admittedly it is a vehicle that changes color from time to time. There is much we do and do not know about dreams, just as there is much we do and do not know about the human brain.

What Do We Know About Dreams?

First, it's important to note that, as with the discussion about consciousness itself, there's a real debate in science as to just what dreams are. There are many, many ideas, hypotheses, theories, and suppositions, and some of them appear to work when placed into practical application or as part of experimentation. There are, however, many missing pieces to the puzzling existence of the dreamworld and how we tie into it. We don't even have complete information on how the brain works, let alone what this thing we call mind or consciousness is.

In the non-psychic world, dreams fall into three broad categories. *Manifest* dreams are what we remember—the normal dreams or nightmares that impinge on our conscious mind. Of course, people have been able to train themselves to make more of their dreams manifest in their memories, to remember more of them. *Latent* dreams are those that address our unconscious thoughts and wishes. *Lucid* dreams are those in which the dreamer awakens in the dreamscape, aware that he or she is dreaming and capable, if he or she so desires, of shaping that dreamworld.

Those studying dreams fall into two camps: those who see dreams as being consciousness-related in a way that supports working with them to help understand ourselves better and to apply what we learn in a practical manner, and those who fall into the more materialist/mechanistic view of consciousness with dreaming as a way to essentially clean up extraneous stuff in our brains. Computer geeks might say this second view is that dreaming defrags our brain, freeing up needed space and function.

The Shape of Our Dreams

In most models of dreaming, there are a number of influences that shape our dreams. Sensory input from the environment around us can affect our dreams. When one is asleep, there is still some sensory scanning of the environment happening. Even though our eyes are shut, our hearing, smelling, and sense of touch are still operating (as is our sense of taste, but that would usually only pick up the taste of the inside of our own mouths … as awful as that might be after a few hours sleep). An alarm clock that didn't wake us up might become a telephone in a dream, an elbow in the back from the person in bed with you transforms in a dream into a knife, a whiff of cologne or perfume becomes a field of flowers. Any odd noises, such as the house settling, the water heater or heat coming on and shutting off, the cat or dog sneaking around (and making noise while doing it) can become a stimulus for some specific event in a dream. However, this is likely to be a very small influence on our dream content, given the rich material available to our brains through memory.

Of course, daily conflicts or stress-inducing events can be translated into the dream, during which we're looking for some kind of conflict resolution. A problem at work can be played out to conclusion in a dream or hidden as part of a kind of mental fable with its own moral.

Movies, TV, and literature can affect what we dream. How many times in your life have you heard (from parents, friends, spouses, etc.) that the scary movie you're watching will give you nightmares—and it does? Anything that stimulates our emotions and thought processes while conscious to the degree a really good horror—or comedy, romance, or science fiction—film, show, or book can is almost certainly the kind of stimulus that will affect our dreams, as it may even affect the content of our daydreams (if you're prone to daydreaming, that is).

Another form of outside stimulus is information brought into your mind through psychic abilities. If we are truly capable of receiving information from the minds of others and from the environment as many believe (telepathy and clairvoyance, respectively), then it follows that this information is just as likely to influence our dreams. Since parapsychologists have found that our conscious belief and disbelief in psychic functioning can have an affect on how psychic we are (disbelievers tending to block out psychic information), and since during the dreaming process our guards are dropped, there is a good opportunity for psychic information to be pulled into dreams and incorporated into them. This added information provides more raw material for whatever the mechanism is in us that creates dreams and their content. With all that information stored in our long-term memories, we can tap quite well into things we know but didn't remember we know.

Our own past experience, that which is locked in our memories, can bring forth an enormous source of raw content for dreams. There is quite a lot we experience in our conscious exploits that we are unaware of. Our senses continuously scan the environment, while our minds focus on particular things to which we pay attention. We truly are unaware of all of the information the memory retains out of everything that our ears hear and our eyes see, yet this is accessible in our dreams and by our intuition.

There seems to be a relaxing of the ingrained censorship of our conscious thought processes during sleep, thus allowing impulses and information from the subconscious to slip through into the dream. According to some experts, many instinctual impulses that may be infantile in nature can come through, as well as impulses that may be ancestral or simply ingrained into the human animal. More to the point of psychic dreaming, the dropping of the rules of the world we use when awake allows for more potential psychic happenings.

How Much?

During the sleep process, we all tend to dream a certain amount. The ratio of time spent dreaming to that of straight sleep changes from the time we are born through adulthood. Newborns may dream as much as 80 percent of the time they are asleep, though generally closer to 50 percent. Children may dream between 30 percent and 40 percent and adults a mere 20 percent to 30 percent. It would seem that as we grow, as our minds get filled with other information, the need for dreaming, for creative but internally suggested information, decreases to less than 20 percent of the time we spend sleeping. How much we *think* we dream may be a function more of how much we can remember dreams rather than how much we actually dream. We do dream every night that we enter rapid eye movement (REM) sleep.

During REM sleep, the eyeballs move from side to side and sometimes up and down, indicating activity in the brain. In addition, there is paralysis of the limbs and irregularity in the heartbeat and respiration. It is in this state, what Stephen LaBerge of Stanford University calls *active sleep*, that we dream. The brain may be more active during this sleep state than at some times when we are awake. According to experts, humans begin dreaming in the womb, as early as the twenty-third week of fetal development.

During REM sleep, the nerve connections that allow and control movement of the body essentially shut down for our own protection. This temporary sleep paralysis prevents us from moving to act out what we experience in our dreams (to keep us from hurting ourselves). We come out of this state of nonmovement fairly quickly, though there are times when the paralysis may take a bit of time to wear off. If you have ever woken up feeling as though you could not move—or even feel—an arm or a leg, you've experienced it. It's also this slow or incomplete coming-out-of sleep paralysis condition that causes some people to feel like there is someone sitting on their chests. In the past, this was often called the "Old Hag" phenomenon, and these days—thanks to bad information propagated by paranormal reality shows—people erroneously conclude there's a spirit (or worse, a demon) attacking. Those who sleepwalk tend to do it in the non-REM stages of sleep, rather than while dreaming, as one might expect. We do know dreaming is absolutely necessary to our own sanity, as is sleep.

To Sleep …

Sleep is thought to be a survival mechanism developed in mammals millions of years ago, due to the higher brain functioning and bodily requirements that mammals have. It is more than simply our bodies requiring rest, since there are other ways besides sleep to get rest. In addition, given the pattern of activity in the brain during sleep, sleep must be more than just a rest-inducing function for mammals. According to Dr. J. Allan Hobson in his book *The Dreaming Brain* (page 288): "…we can fairly assume that it will be difficult to establish any functional hypothesis convincingly because the mechanisms of sleep are only beginning to be understood at the cellular and molecular level."

In general, mammals such as human beings are on a biological clock setting that creates a day pattern for us that works out to approximately twenty-four hours, though some mammals are on a lunar and tidal period of 24.8 hours. Our rhythm of the day has us needing wake time and sleep time at an approximate ratio of two to one, which means that we should sleep about eight hours of every twenty-four. While most people play around with the amount of time spent sleeping, most experts agree that between seven and a half and eight hours are about right to give the body the amount of sleep it needs.

We often hear we *need* less sleep as we grow older, often because of the observation of the amount of time spent sleeping by infants being so much greater than that of adults. However, while it is true that human infants need more sleep, older children and adults (of any age) need about the same amount of sleep. What happens as we get older is that our patterns change to accommodate scheduling for things like work and leisure activities. We tend to sleep less during the week when we have to get up for work than on the weekends when we don't. Many people (myself included) use the days off to "catch up on sleep." Unfortunately, many experts agree that catching up really doesn't work that way (although sleeping an extra few hours on weekends sure feels good to me).

Sleep appears to be rest not only for the body but also a necessary change in brain patterns and activity. Some have suggested that it allows for processing information to aid memory and learning of the day's events. While our ancestors saw sleep as a shutdown of bodily functions and even a state akin to death, the research results we do have about sleep indicate that it allows for both physiological and psychological housekeeping to go on.

Sleep Deprivation

Studies of sleep deprivation indicate some personality alteration the longer the person is awake beyond simple change in behavior because the individual is tired. Sleep deprivation seems to undermine decision-making ability, especially where creativity is concerned. We (most of us) apparently need at least five hours of sleep per night to avoid a loss of such creative abilities and to avoid some degree of forgetfulness. Of course, there are some people whose body clocks allow them the need for less sleep and there are those who need more than the "normal" amount to be able to function well.

With increased hours of sleep deprivation may come some degree of paranoia and irrational judgment and behavior. In fact, prolonged wakefulness can lead to hallucinations—daymares that are more rightly related to REM-state imagery. Finally, some studies show that some individuals may exhibit psychotic behavior patterns if deprived of sleep for 100 hours or more.

In studies looking at REM deprivation, where the individuals are awakened the moment they enter REM in order to abort the REM state (and therefore dreaming), the person's system generally attempts to get to REM as soon as the individual goes back to sleep. Lengthy deprivation of REM sleep/dreaming may lead to waking dreams (hallucinations). When the dream-deprived individual can get back into the REM state, it may be a lengthy period of dreaming, as though the individual was dream-starved and binges on dreaming when allowed to.

States and Stages of Sleep

We go through a total of four stages of sleep a number of times (cycles) throughout a typical sleep period, though there is often a fuzzy line between the two deepest levels of sleep. From the time we are awake until we hit the first stage, we are often in a pre-sleep stage called the *hypnagogic state.* This is a state in which body muscles are loose and we feel very relaxed, with people often reporting the sensation of floating. It is in this state that we often can hear noises in our homes and exaggerate them into imaginary burglars or disasters. It is in this state that our waking consciousness is a little fuzzy and may wander, daydream in effect. And it is in this hypnagogic state that OBEs often take place. In fact, some of the techniques talked about by people purporting to teach astral projection may be relaxation techniques that lead to a hypnagogic state, and therefore may actually yield real OBEs and not mere psychological experiences.

Once we pass by this pre-sleep state, we enter stage one of sleep —a light-sleeping stage that we re-enter later as our REM state. In this first stage, we are more easily awakened. We go past stage one into an intermediate sleep, stage two; we are more relaxed and harder to awaken. We pass through this into stage three, a deep state of sleep, and finally to stage four, the deepest state of non-REM sleep. In this state our bodies are completely relaxed and conserving energy, and we are very difficult to awaken. Animals that hibernate do so in a state like the deepest sleep we enter into, where their bodily functions are conserving energy for perhaps months at a time.

After a time, we leave the deeper states of sleep and head back up to stage one and enter REM sleep; the whole cycle taking about ninety minutes. In a typical night, we enter REM sleep four or five times, with the REM period becoming longer as sleep continues uninterrupted. In a typical seven- to eight-hour sleep period, approximately 50 percent of our dreaming falls into the last two hours of sleep. This means that if we cut our sleep short, we may have less time dreaming as the longer REM sleep periods are cut off.

It was in 1953 that Eugene Aserinsky and Nathaniel Kleitman of the University of Chicago distinguished the REM sleep state. William Dement, working under Kleitman, continued the important work that connected REM sleep with dreaming. It was discovered that when you wake a person up during the REM stage of sleep, they will report dreaming 85 percent of the time. In 1957, Dement and Kleitman introduced the criteria for sleep stages. In 1959, Michel Jouvet and Francois Michel of Lyon, France, first published their observations of the inhibition of muscle tone related to the paralysis in REM sleep.

Sleep Disorders

It is in the deepest levels of sleep that sleep disorders such as night terrors and sleepwalking—somnambulism—occur. It is estimated that between two and seven million Americans might have a less than *good* night's sleep, being bothered by sleep disorders of one form or another. Besides night terror and sleepwalking, these disorders include sleep talking, narcolepsy, insomnia, teeth grinding, bedwetting, and sleep apnea.

In stages three and four of sleep, our muscular system is not paralyzed as it is in REM sleep. The body may respond, while we are asleep, to particular orders to move around, talk, or experience intense fears (as in night terrors). Sleep talking may be a disorder some people suffer from, with the sleep talker generally making little sense and not capable of any sort of conversation as the brain has little activity, as it would in REM sleep (although I did have a roommate in college who answered questions intelligibly, and honestly—unfortunately for him—he may have been in REM at the time, since he did recall dreaming some of the conversations).

Sleep*walkers* generally do not move around too much, unlike what we see in some comedy films. Many also suffer from night terrors, and the movements made during the sleepwalk may be related to the night terror being experienced. Sleepwalkers may do a bit of sleep talking at the time they move about. There are exceptional cases of activity during sleepwalking. Some sleepwalkers have been known to get out of bed and head for the kitchen. Sleep eaters, who generally don't suffer from waking eating disorders, often wake to find their kitchens messed up, with evidence that they ate quite a bit during the night. Activity such as this has been reported as a side effect of certain pharmaceutical sleep aids.

In rare cases, otherwise fairly nonviolent people may commit an act of extreme violence in their sleep. In a legal case in the 1980s, a man in Toronto was acquitted from a murder charge on the basis that he was sleepwalking at the time. He had (sleep) driven several miles to where his in-laws lived and killed his mother-in-law and almost killed his father-in-law. He then ended up turning himself in to the police with the claim that he was sleepwalking at the time (horrified, apparently, at what he had done in his sleep).

He was found innocent by the jury after evidence of his personal history of sleepwalking was revealed, along with observations of his sleepwalking while he was in jail. Physical examination provided evidence of brain-wave patterns indicative of sleepwalkers. This sort of violence is extremely rare, fortunately.

REM Behavior Disorder

There is a movement-related disorder that occurs during REM sleep. REM sleep behavior disorder covers people who apparently physically act out their dreams, the paralysis of the body that normally accompanies REM sleep not working for them. Sufferers of the disorder apparently move about, sometimes violently so, during occurrence of their dreams. Spouses or others have been injured when they have been present during such occurrences of dream-induced movements. Studies of this disorder indicate that most of the sufferers are men, generally older than fifty, though some children have experienced the disorder as well.

Sleep Apnea

Another non-REM disorder is sleep apnea, which relates to restricted breathing or stopping breathing during sleep. This disorder affects the throat muscles, which tend to relax so much as to close off breathing. The discomfort and problem of the brain and body not getting enough oxygen generally cause the sleeper to wake up just enough so that the connections between brain and throat muscles are reinstated, causing them to work again. Such awakenings can disrupt sleep enough to cause the individual to be prone to sleepiness during waking hours.

Insomnia

Millions of people suffer from insomnia of one form or another, having difficulty in either getting to sleep or in staying asleep. They may wake up continually through the night or may wake up too early and not be able to get back to sleep.

Temporary insomnia may be a result of stress, worries, or even excitement in our daily lives. Such stresses and worries that keep us awake may simply relate to worrying about getting to sleep in the first place. For many, a self-perpetuating cycle of insomnia can occur when they worry, after not being able to get to sleep, whether they can get to sleep at all. You can't sleep, so you worry about not sleeping, the worrying keeping you from sleeping, which continues the insomnia. Dealing with the stresses that may cause such temporary insomnia will usually rid us of the insomnia.

In addition, sleeping too much can affect us adversely. For example, sleeping very late on a Sunday morning (maybe into the early afternoon) may result in difficulty getting to sleep early on Sunday night (early because you have to work the next day).

Chronic insomnia may be a result of poor sleep habits or irregular sleep patterns. Perhaps the insomniac's sleep pattern is not a regular ninety-minute pattern in and out of the cycles. Or perhaps the person suffers from a sleep-phase syndrome, in which the body's internal clock is out of phase with what we consider ordinary sleep patterns, sleeping at night (they just can't sleep at night, because their biological clocks have them on a schedule where they ought to be awake at night and asleep during the day).

Drugs such as sleeping pills are often used by people to get to sleep when insomnia strikes. Unfortunately, that can lead to drug dependency insomnia, where one cannot sleep without first taking the drug. Often there are simple ways to deal with insomnia, from relaxation and meditative techniques to simply staying out of bed for any reason other than sleep (and sex, of course). Too often the bed becomes a place of activity, from reading to watching television, and not just a place for sleeping. Making the major activity association between the bed and sleep seems to help a great deal in overcoming sleeplessness. Finally, adopting a regular schedule of sleep and waking time may reduce any unfortunate insomnia. For those suffering from sleep-phase syndrome, altering their schedules (so they are awake at night and asleep during the day) seems to work well.

Narcolepsy

An opposite sleep disorder from insomnia is that of narcolepsy, in which one tends to fall asleep at often inappropriate (and sometimes dangerous) times. This disorder, which appears to be genetically related, may afflict more than a quarter of a million people in this country alone. Narcoleptics may fall asleep at work, at the wheel of a car, in a movie, or even during sexual intercourse. They may have a different pattern to their sleep, falling asleep for short periods of time and often immediately into the REM state, and may also tend to have hallucinations. Narcolepsy can be treated through the use of stimulants.

Sleep Pattern Disruption

Finally, humans may have problematic sleep patterns due to post-traumatic stress syndrome. Dreams and other reactions related to this syndrome can be merely symptoms of the syndrome which, according to therapists, should be addressed by working through the trauma. Other forms of anxiety dreams similar to post-traumatic, stress-induced dreams may play a key role in helping us to recover from emotional wounds (from relationship problems, grief due to death of a loved one, problems with work) other than those as dramatic as the physical events that cause the syndrome (such as seeing someone killed, being raped, living through a devastating natural disaster, and so on).

Dreams as Body-Health Indicators

Dreams are often indicators of physical as well as psychological stresses. In various studies, including one by Dr. Robert Smith of Michigan State University, it's been indicated that content and themes of dreams may reflect health problems. A study of cardiac patients showed that those with worse heart disease had more dreams involving incidents of death or separation from family. Looking at our dreams may lead us to uncover physical ailment pointers. Part of us may be better able to recognize the signs of physical illness than our conscious minds and may play out those diagnoses in our dreams. In addition, our dreams give us access to important emotional issues in our lives, which could in turn affect our physical health.

Dreams may also have positive effects on the physical body. Studies of visualization techniques with healing indicate that such techniques may positively affect the body's pattern of healing. Dealing with illness in dreams may create a physical effect. Evidence indicates that visualized rehearsal of physical movements, from dance to sleight of hand, may at some level prepare the muscles for such activities. Dreams may yield physical solutions to problems, as evidenced by athletes like golfer Jack Nicklaus who dreamed a solution to a bad golf swing. Lucid dream studies with sexual activity going on in the dream state reveal physical arousal in the dreamer as though the dream sex were a real, objective experience.

Creativity

Dreams are often essential to the creative mind as well. Many people, from scientists to artists to writers to businessmen, have found themselves in the position of having a dream offer them the bit of information that allows them to say "Eureka! I've got it!" after having worked on a problem consciously for too long with no result. Even the saying "I'll sleep on it" indicates this. There are examples of this throughout history, from Robert Louis Stevenson taking *The Strange Case of Dr. Jekyll and Mr. Hyde* from a dream to Friedrich Kekule coming up with the structure of the benzene ring due to dream imagery. We might not have the sewing machine from Elias Howe if not for dreams.

Symbolism

Sigmund Freud saw dreams as wish fulfillment. In latent dreams, our repressed feelings or unconscious desires and conflicts may show through strongly. Freud, like many since, felt that desires and feelings are often so threatening to our conscious minds that they need to be represented in disguised form so as to not directly arouse a person's conscience. Symbolism is heavily at play in Freud's dreamworld; things are not what they seem. A single character or object can represent many, and the most important emotions or messages of a dream may be reintegrated in a safe or seemingly unimportant image. Freud's analysis of dreams dealt with sexual images, as did much of his psychoanalytic imagery process, and often symbols were the same for all dreamers.

On the other hand, Carl Jung felt that there are no fixed symbolic meanings for all people with the exception of a few very basic archetypes. One must take each person separately, studying that person's dreams over a period of time, to get a handle on that particular person's system of symbols, he thought. This is how many dreamwork groups operate today.

The Problem of Recall and Reconstruction

One basic problem with the process of working with dreams is that we have a tendency to reorganize and elaborate on a dream while remembering it—to make it more logical and add to it so that it makes sense to our conscious minds.

This is a problem we also have in dealing with our own psychic experiences. As a psychic image or information piece comes into our minds, we immediately want to categorize what it is we are seeing or hearing with our psychic sense. If our mind gets a sudden picture of something, rather than taking it at face value, we seem to have to identify it with something we already know, as though we need to make that image symbolic of something already in our experience. What is unfortunate here is that often the psychic information is about something new to our experience, and there is little to be used if we fit the new information into an old category.

Time in the Dream State

Research indicates that the length of dream time approximates the actual waking time or clock time of the nondreaming, outside world. Of course, many of us apparently remember dreams that seem to cover weeks, months, or even years of time, leading to what is apparently a false conclusion (if experimental evidence is correct) that dreams compress time, so that minutes or hours of subjective dreaming pass by in a matter of seconds of real time while dreaming. Stephen LaBerge and others have suggested that such dreams use similar imagery and plot devices as films and television programs do to show that time passes (hopefully minus commercials), such as perhaps fading to black then fading back to a morning image immediately to indicate that a night has passed, or even the flipping of calendar pages to indicate many days, weeks, or months passing, something I remember from dreams of my own.

In the REM state, the eyes often move back and forth in the same pattern they do in a dream. A recollected dream of the observation of a tennis match will generally yield the same back and forth pattern as what is remembered from the dream. LaBerge conducted experiments with communicating from the lucid dream state in which he was to move his eyes in that dream in a particular pattern at a certain time after beginning to dream. Others have reported using a code with regards to eye movements in the dream state to actually send messages to the waking world. Eye movements can indicate the start and finish of a count of time (say ten seconds) and can be compared by an observer with clock time.

The Waking World Affects Our Dreams

Dreams tend to reflect current issues in our lives, and they may be excellent mood reflectors as well. Our mood right before sleep may directly affect the content and quality of our dreams, and our dreams during the night may affect how we wake up and in what mood. Other stimuli such as movies or TV, fantasizing, or neighborhood or household noise occurring before we head for sleep might also affect dream content, specifically the emotional feel of the dream.

Our perceptions of the real world while awake during the day also appear to affect our dreams directly. Experiments with people wearing colored glasses or goggles often yield dreams with those colors showing predominantly. Looking at the world through rose-colored glasses may result in dreams of rose-colored imagery.

We usually talk of dreams in terms of imagery—of visual information—but blind people also dream, though generally with the auditory being the overwhelming mode of mental imagery. People not born blind but who later lose their sight stick with the visual, though there is evidence that indicates that this peters out down the line in favor of the sense now most relied on (hearing). Dreams are typically composed of the visual and the auditory, though some people do report other senses sometimes having a say in the dreams. In this we see that dreams are tied most closely to the waking senses we rely on. This may depend on which neurons are firing during the dreaming (those related to the visual system of the brain, the auditory, or otherwise).

Perception vs. Sense

It's interesting to note that psychic experience is very similar, with visual-form information predominant in the experiences, to how we process information from our other senses. Most people experience psychic information as visual imagery through the mind's eye, though some may lean toward the information being presented as a sound perception (the mind's ear?) or through feeling and touch or even smell.

As an example, if a group of people likely to have psychic experiences enters a haunted house, a place where there is much history, some people might report seeing a ghost that the others don't visually perceive. A couple might experience a cold chill or the sense that someone has touched them on the shoulder or arm when there's no one there. Some others might hear the sound of footsteps down an empty hallway, and still others might seemingly smell perfume or cologne or something not so nice. If there were attempts to record what was seen or heard, nothing is typically what you'd get. The stimulus of the psychic information appears to cause the mind/brain to respond with appropriate images, more or less as hallucinations with outside causes.

So, we tend to perceive things in dreams or in psychic experience with much the same hierarchy of senses as we do with our waking perceptions. Since sight is the sense most relied on by the majority of us, that's the modality we use most in dreams. Most people do dream in color, but we sometimes forget the color schemes, and the dream might then be incorrectly remembered as having been in black and white. This does not preclude us from having dreams in black and white. In fact, I can remember a couple of my own dreams where I was watching a film or a television show that was in black and white (although everything but the film/show was in color). I have also heard from friends and acquaintances that they have occasionally dreamed they were part of an old movie scenario, and that it appeared to have been a black-and-white dream (it obviously hadn't been colorized yet).

Dreams appear to range from the incredibly exciting and utterly fantastic to images that approximate or appear to be real events—but are not, in fact, true events that have happened to you—to replays of real, daily events which may be very, very boring. It's possible that some of the experiences we have that we call déjà vu, where we could almost swear we've been through a situation or to a place before, are actually situations where the real event triggers a half-remembered reality-approximating dream. You may even have a dream coming close to reality that you forget was a dream, one you integrate as a real memory.

Why Do We Dream? Meaning vs. Mechanism

There are many ideas about the functions and forms of dreams, and many of these are often at great odds with the ideas of the pioneers of psychology and psychoanalysis and with each other.

Some researchers and theorists in recent times do see dreams as that channel to understanding yourself. Gayle Delaney, director of the Delaney & Flowers Dream and Consultation Center in San Francisco, sees dreams as something like poetry, with metaphors created by the brain/mind representing real information and emotions.

Dreams can help resolve problems and integrate change into our lives, or they can be unhealthy, keeping us dwelling on past problems without a chance of resolution. The content of dreams tends to vary according to issues in your own life, as well as issues in the world around you. Dreams may be dramatizations of hidden feelings. They may show us these feelings that we refuse to consciously acknowledge, and they may provide detail as to the reasons behind these feelings. What most tend to agree on today is that the symbols in dreams are not absolutes, unlike what many of those dream analysis books would have you believe. They are not the same for all people, although there may be themes that are common to many. Recurring dreams may simply be recurring because they reveal issues you are avoiding or not addressing while awake.

According to LaBerge, dreams help us work through ways of interacting with the world and our expectations of it. In our dreams we can address how to get what we want and avoid what we don't want, although the messages/answers provided may be symbolic or metaphorical, or they may be as plain as writing on the wall.

Dreams may simply occur to entertain us. They don't necessarily have to be windows into the unconscious or filled with exceedingly important messages. They could simply replay a film you just saw or dramatize a book or short story you just read (how many of you have had *Star Trek* dreams? Or am I the only one?).

Brain as Mechanism

From the *mechanistic* perspective of neuroscience, dreams may simply occur to keep circuits of the brain ready and able for the intellectual challenges of the next day. Neuroscientists often have very straightforward ways of looking at REM sleep and dreaming. Robert Vertes sees REM sleep as helping to keep us alive, acting as the brain's "pilot light" during sleep. In 1987, Jonathan Winson of the Rockefeller University discussed the idea that dreaming helps with information processing of stuff we can't get through while awake. Consider it off-line processing of information through the brain's computer center, with the online processing being conducted during waking hours.

In the early 1980s, Francis Crick (the unraveler of DNA) and Graeme Mitchison of Cambridge University brought in the theory that dreams are not necessarily worth remembering, that such recalling may be hazardous to our (mental) health. They see dreams as the way the brain/mind fine-tunes itself, flushing out the extraneous garbage we pick up while awake. In dreaming, the mind detects and unlearns or tries to forget this unwanted, unneeded information. The brain is working in REM as a sorting mechanism, deciding what to save to the hard disk of your mind (long-term memory) and what is junk to toss out (short-term memory, soon forgotten). By this notion, it's easy to see that remembering such stuff could be detrimental to our normal functioning.

If this sounds like the workings of a computer, that's fine, since the brain is at least metaphorically that. Christopher Evans, author of *Landscapes of the Night,* takes that analogy and puts it to good use. In large-scale computer systems, where there is an enormous amount of information added on any given day, there is often a need to "take the system down" or off-line to add bulks of information, update files, scan for errors, do system building, and process that information and integrate it into the system's architecture. One might consider the brain as a computer, looking at REM sleep and dreaming as that off-line time period, given that normal body and brain functions are not going on at the time. As with a computer system, the normal demands on the system are shut out in sleep, allowing for some time periods (REM sleep) to process information and build/rebuild the system. Such a process may happen in a single REM session or extend over many periods if the issue or information being dealt with requires extensive attention.

In dreams, information gathered during the day may be compared and contrasted with information gathered in the past and stored in permanent, long-term memory. Some information may be similar to duplicate files in a computer, and therefore may be processed out of existence, or at least out of our conscious minds. Some may be erased, as with perhaps some of the unnecessary garbage Crick and Mitchison talk about.

In the Brain

During REM sleep, there is activity in the brain stem that stimulates particular neurons using the chemical neurotransmitter acetylcholine. Neurons using acetylcholine are effectively *on* during REM sleep, while the neurotransmitters serotonin and norepinephrine are *off* during REM (and on during non-REM sleep). The random firings of the neurons during REM are interpreted by the cortex of the brain and woven into some kind of story to make some sense of the signals received. There is an indication that acetylcholine is related directly to dreaming, as injections of a similar chemical into animals yields REM sleep in those animals.

J. Allan Hobson of Harvard University has suggested that we forget our dreams not because they are meant to be forgotten, but because they are stored in short-term, rather than long-term memory (norepinephrine and serotonin, which are not being produced in REM sleep, are necessary for long-term memory). To continue the computer analogy, in dreams some (perhaps all) of the information is squeezed onto what I'll call flash (or thumb) drive memory rather than saved to the "hard disk" of long-term memory.

In other words, dreaming and REM sleep may be signs of processing of information, and therefore directly related to learning. The mechanism of REM sleep may stimulate higher centers of the brain, thereby having the functions of maintaining the central nervous system and helping it develop in children. Michel

Jouvet of the University of Lyon proposed that during dreaming, we are practicing, rehearsing, trying out instinctual or genetically programmed behaviors in a state in which our bodies are effectively paralyzed, and so without consequence. Such rehearsal may work for you in a physical way, as mentioned earlier, in getting your muscles ready for an unfamiliar activity. This may be why we dream so much in early stages of our lives and find there is a decrease of amount of time spent in REM and dreaming sleep when we become older.

To take the maintenance idea a step further, Dr. Ian Oswald of the University of Edinburgh has postulated that REM sleep occurs to allow the central nervous system to make repair to worn-down brain tissue and connections. During non-REM sleep, growth hormones are released that repair the body. REM sleep allows for the same to be done for the brain, with dreams occurring as a by-product.

REM sleep may be an evolutionary development of a mechanism needed to keep the brain efficiently operating. The brain may be processing information in REM and through dreams, and may be using this special state of activity to keep brain tissue in good working order, or as Oswald suggests, to repair it.

Affecting Our Dreams

We know that both the body and the mind affect dreaming. Physical condition can affect the occurrence of REM sleep, as well as provide cues for the content and themes of dreams. Our physical state when we go to sleep may affect dreams, as well. While eating unhealthy food or too much food may not cause bad dreams and nightmares, it may affect our dreams and their content because of the ways our bodies and neurochemistry are affected by that food. The positions in which we sleep and whether we experience any cramping may affect the content of our dreams, and any signals from the outside, from an alarm clock going off to a siren from a fire engine to an earth tremor, may cause a reaction in our dreams. Alcohol and drugs can affect our dreams, though they tend to decrease or even suppress REM sleep and dreaming.

The mind and what we think and feel affects dreaming. Emotional feelings and moods affect our dreams, and intentions and expectations also come into play. Verbal messages and expressions heard during the day may be translated into visual imagery in dreams. According to Dr. Rosalind Cartwright of the Rush-Presbyterian-St. Luke's Medical Center in Chicago, in an interview in Health magazine (July 1989): "Dreams perform important emotional homework.... They review and revise our concept of who we are and rehearse where we are going. When life is tough, dreams provide a mechanism for repair."

We are still at the beginning of the pathway toward understanding the mind/brain connection in ourselves, and we know less than we'd like to admit. Where psychic experiences and their place within our own functioning are concerned, we know very little and in fact a lot less than what we know about sleep and dreams. Psychic experiences are, unlike dreams, less than accepted in many societies, and have yet to be tied to a particular physical or mental state. Experimentation on psychic abilities moves on, with some research now being conducted in connecting such activity (if it even goes on within the biological framework) to particular areas of the brain, thanks to new techniques in brain mapping, such as magnetic resonance imaging and neuromagnetic mapping—using magnetic fields and computers to create a fuller, more highly defined picture of activity and structure in the body and brain.

Physiologically based studies of both dreams and psychic functioning may eventually yield the definites of such mechanisms, the how of those activities, but such studies may never yield the why. If, as many propose, dreams are a by-product of brain activity, this does leave the intentional dream or the lucid dream as real gray areas, since we have no answer at the moment.

Dissent from the Dreamworkers

Not many dreamworkers go along with a purely mechanistic view of dreams and the brain, as the overwhelming majority find the recall and working through of dreams as a valuable, practical process with many payoffs. Dr. Rosalind Cartwright, for example, believes that the processing of information to include comparison of the day's events with past memory occurs to put the information into perspective, to bring it in line with the personality of the individual. The practical application of dreamwork, which requires remembering one's dreams, has shown value time and again. I fully support this perspective.

Bridging the Two Camps

Providing somewhat of a bridge between the two approaches is that of J. Allan Hobson of Harvard University. REM sleep (and dreaming) is a survival mechanism to keep the circuits of the brain viable and ready for the non-sleep periods of our life. The brain is randomly firing neurons during REM sleep that may approximate the firing of neurons during the waking stages, and then creates a story in which to place the actions that would normally result from the firing of those same neurons. Hobson puts forward the idea that the content can be read directly, rather than considered more symbolic of deep-seated wishes and issues that many consider the cause of the dreams. Brain activity, not psychological issues, cause dreaming and often the form of the dreams. Excessive firings of the neurons related to our optic system cause more visual dreams. Hobson suggests that the brain may be creative in its storylines for the dreams, and even just plain entertaining. Dreams may be simply there to be used for amusement, or may reflect some inner issues. Much of what we remember or make of our dreams may occur after the dream, using waking logic to construct something that makes sense to our conscious minds.

REM sleep, according to Hobson in *The Dreaming Brain*, may fulfill its place in us as a sort of maintenance program, even aiding in our development as human beings as we grow up. "Early in development, REM sleep could provide the brain with a highly organized program of internal action. This program is stereotyped, redundant, and reliable—all features useful to a developing system (page 292)."

According to Stephen LaBerge, this "activation synthesis model" may explain the physiological *how* we dream, but not the psychological *why* we dream (or why we dream *what* we dream). There is the added problem of lucid dreams, where we are effectively conscious in our dreams, indicating signals and information processing in the REM state that is anything but random.

Since your body is effectively paralyzed during REM sleep, the firing of the same neurons that could otherwise result in walking or picking something up would create signals that can be the basis of the same or similar action in a dream. The dream, then, is truly a representation or metaphor or acting out, but it is one of the impulses of the nervous system, rather than solely based on what is in your conscious or unconscious. Most of the outside sensory input is tuned out, but that which gets by might be incorporated with the dream. Finally, the story created might be added to by extraneous information the brain can pull from memory (otherwise we might simply have a pretty dull story). Effectively, the brain takes what might otherwise (in your state of REM paralysis) be meaningless, mental static and uses it as the building blocks of a dream.

As you can see by this little peek at some of the ideas surrounding sleep and dreams, there are a number of ideas, though many of them seem to be able to work together to form a larger picture of brain/mind functioning.

Dream Recall

Assuming, as I do, there's a positive reason to work with dreams, how can we do that if we can't remember them? The answer is that you can *learn to remember* your dreams and can even learn to program them to deal with certain issues and problems (or for entertainment value), or to become lucid dreams in which anything goes and you're in control. According to many who have learned to work with their own dreams (and learned to remember them first), something as simple as the interest level in your dreams and the intent to remember them can help that recall process. In fact, from the time I started writing this book, I began spontaneously to remember my own dreams more than I think I ever have since college.

LaBerge and others say that you can program yourself to remember your dreams. The issue of belief and intention, in believing you *can* and intending to remember them, is very important here. If you doubt you can remember, you may never learn to do that. Belief versus doubt is of essence in many areas of human endeavor, from performance in sports to having psychic experiences. Intention, interest, and willingness to believe will affect the recall of dreams. More on this later in the book.

Using Our Dreams

Once we've begun to recall and sift through our dreams, we can begin to make use of them. We can make suggestions to ourselves before going to bed that may actually affect what we dream, so that we can dream to deal with our everyday problems, to relieve stress, to confront our fears and overcome our nightmares, to entertain ourselves, to enhance our own creativity, to help with decision-making, and to get to know ourselves better.

We may also be able to use dreams for healing our bodies through appropriate imagery that might help speed up our body's healing processes, and for healing our minds through dealing with the underlying issues that may cause us to be psychologically distraught, unstable, or stressed out. Of course, we may use our dreams as vehicles for psychic connections with those around us and with our own environment, scanning both our past experiences and perhaps other points in time and space with psychic ability for the information needed to complete a dream scenario.

Throughout the rest of this book we will look further at that last possibility, that we are not only dealing with our own internal experiences, as psychic abilities provide other connections we make with the world outside our minds, awake and dreaming.

chapter 3
Dream On: The Form of Your Dreams

Dreams often have an overriding theme or feel to them, whether positive, neutral, or negative. For the most part, during the dream we are totally unaware we are dreaming, though lucid dreams are the exception to that. We wake up sometimes with recollection of the specifics of the dream and sometimes just with a general good or bad (or no) feeling. It's the bad dreams, the ones with negative emotion or imagery that often impact us the most.

The Dark Side: Nightmares and Daymares

Imagine for a moment that a world leader is concerned about the escalating possibility of a terrorist getting his hands on a nuclear weapon. The leader's sleep is fitful and most of his dreams center around the theme of a nuclear attack on his home city. This nightmare is recurrent, always with high emotion, and he finds himself not wanting to sleep because of it. Sleep deprivation and the emotion he carries with him when he has the nightmares brings questions to the minds of those around him as to whether he is still capable of using good judgment to make decisions as a leader. And still the nightmares persist.

The real possibility of nuclear war has given more than a few people nightmares. In fact, there have been reports of children having such bad dreams. In today's world, with increasing fears of both foreign and homegrown terrorists and mass shootings, more and more people may be having bad dreams expressing their real-life anxieties and fears. Nightmares in general have often been described as dreams in which our waking fears have gone wild.

But is that all they are? Do nightmares only have to do with the real, overt fears we face in our waking lives? Let's explore the "dark side" of dreams for a bit.

The origins of the word *nightmare* betray ideas of what people thought these extremely vivid, but terrifying, dreams were: "night demons" or "night goblins" or "night spirits," depending on who you talk to. All relate to the idea that the nightmare was thought to have been caused by evil spirits or supernatural creatures coming into our dreams while we were asleep at night. Children, not being very strong-willed, were considered prime targets for such demons. As children tend to have many more bad dreams than adults, that idea was borne out by simple observation. Or should I say that it was likely that the idea came about because children experience more nightmares and therefore are better targets for the night spirits that invade our dreams?

Then there's that old wives' tale (not so old ... you still hear it today) that nightmares are caused by eating too much of a good thing (too many sweets, for example) or by eating the wrong thing, more or less our body's way of seeking revenge for stretching the stomach lining a bit too much. More likely, it's the alteration of brain chemistry caused by certain foods' affects on individuals.

Dreams of Disaster ... Dreams of Monsters

Many experts see nightmares as very intense dreams that play out some of our childhood fears and feelings of anxiety, others as dealing with the common fears, the archetypal fears, that all people face. And there are several types of nocturnal incidents that people call nightmares. The biggest split between two types of sleep-related terrifying incidents that occur is that between *night terrors* and *nightmares.*

Night Terrors

Night terrors are situations in which we wake up, often covered with a cold sweat (missing from reactions to most nightmares), realizing we're terrified but not remembering why or whether it was because of a dream. In fact, it is very likely that we don't even wake up fully from a night terror, and we may scream, move about in bed, or even sleepwalk a bit due to the night terror. It occurs in the early part of the sleep period, and during non-REM stages of sleep, when we are not only not paralyzed, but *not dreaming.*

Night terrors and nightmares are experienced more frequently by children than by adults, and it appears that most of us outgrow these experiences. Both may be experienced by adults, but generally adults, on average, may only have a nightmare a couple of times a year, with night terrors less frequent than that. Night terrors occur sometime within one to three hours after falling asleep, usually in the deepest stage of sleep. Nightmares, although they may happen in just about any REM-sleep period, occur generally in the later hours of the time you are asleep, when the REM stage lasts longer; the longer we sleep, the more the cycle of non-REM/REM reoccurs, the longer the REM stage.

Night terrors are a form of parasomia, sleep disorders that are related to sleepwalking and even grinding your teeth while you sleep. Children who have night terrors often wake up screaming, though they are not fully awake. Parents running into their rooms to see what's wrong may find them hard to calm down, limbs flailing as though the child is trying to escape something, eyes wide open and even glazed looking, and not recognizing that the parents are there, or possibly not recognizing the parents at all. The screaming and the hysterical fear may last more than a few minutes or end as soon as the parents lay the child back down. If the child actually calms down and recognizes the parents, it's as if he/she is just waking up. Asked about what scared the child, he/she has no idea, no recall. Parents might simply think this is a nightmare, or might think, if the situation happens multiple times, that the child has a psychological problem.

In fact, neither is the case. During the night terror, the child is simply *not awake, but still sleeping.* Given that the night terror occurs in the non-REM stages of sleep, the child is truly in the deepest stages of sleep, and may be more difficult to wake up right away after falling back to sleep. In this deepest state of sleep, we can sleep through just about anything, even through our own night terrors. There is no recall of what caused the night terror because the brain activity is very different than REM, from which we can recall imagery and content. We are, during night terrors, not dreaming...not creating signals that might dump into either long- or short-term memory.

Most night terrors occur in very young children, preschoolers according to some experts. They typically occur any time up until about eight years of age, and they may occur in children as young as six months. According to some studies, night terrors occur more frequently in boys than in girls. As we grow up, we tend to outgrow the night terrors; they seem related more to physical activity in the body and brain not related to mind, rather than the physical activity in the brain that stimulates mental processes in REM sleep. In adults, the rare night terror is recognizably a different experience than a nightmare.

A child may not wake at all during the night terror, yet may wake up during a nightmare. With little or no recall of having even had the night terror, there is no comparison to the nightmare. As adults, we may wake up in a cold sweat, our hearts pounding, breathing hard, and knowing we just had *something* happen to us in our sleep, something probably unsettling or even frightening, causing a feeling of terror or panic, but again with no recall of anything but that vague feeling. We can be disoriented and not fully awake, and sometimes not awake at all. We may have flailed our arms a bit, and the night terror might be accompanied by a bit of sleepwalking. It's as if our bodies react to something our minds can't quite get a grasp on, which seems to be exactly the case.

Night terrors may be more indicative of physiological and neurological imbalances than anything psychological, whether in children or adults. Children who are extremely tired may fall into that deepest stage of sleep in which night terrors occur (as might adults, for that matter). Night terrors in adults may be the result of stress, both physical and psychological (though it's been shown that psychological stress can cause physical problems). Unfortunately, night terrors are a part of childhood, although parents may consider them unusual and even worry when they happen more than once or twice. Most children will have at least one night terror as they grow up, but generally more than that. There is some evidence to indicate that frequent night terrors in children are genetically related, that such patterns of repetition of the night terrors run in families. This makes sense, given their physiologically based nature.

Nightmares

A nightmare is a dream with negative content; it occurs during REM sleep and may last more than a few minutes. There are all the qualities of any other dream, though in the nightmare we have particular fears, anxieties, frustrations, and perhaps even guilty feelings coming out. We are generally not able to move about while having a nightmare, being in that induced sleep paralysis that accompanies REM-sleep and all other forms of dreams.

Nightmares provide information, imagery, and emotion as other dreams do. The content of nightmares is often pulled from childhood fears, though one cannot discount the fears adults take on. While we are children, we are effectively both vulnerable (not capable of being fully functional in the world around us) and protected (by our parents). Such feelings of helplessness and vulnerability can cause fear and anxiety in us as children, and they can certainly come up in our dreams as adults, even being related to our adult lives.

Have you ever felt helpless to affect a particular situation in your life, to remedy it to the better, whether that situation revolves around work, around your relationships, around money, and so on? Nightmares are dreams that can play out any helpless feelings, any fears or anxieties, whether relating to our fears or worries of failure or of being physically injured, or even left isolated and alone. Nightmares may be due to actual phobias (phobic nightmares), but they are more often related to happenings in our lives, due to fears of being fired, recent accidents we have had (or seen), divorce, bankruptcy, and other negatives. Nightmares can even betray a fear of success, something that more than a few people experience.

While the majority of the nightmare-type dreams that we have do occur in childhood and we tend to outgrow them as we out-grow night terrors, nightmares do follow us into our adult lives. As mentioned earlier, we tend to have a couple every year, though experts have done studies that contend that one out of every 200 to 500 adults (discrepancy due to different study results) have them as often as once a week.

According to a national survey commissioned in 1982 by ABC Television and the *Washington Post* (Henry Allen, "The American Dreams; Fear of Falling and Other Long National Nightmares" *Washington Post,* July 7, 1982), dreams of falling were the most frequent (71 percent) followed by dreams of seeing a loved one in danger or dead (59 percent) and dreams of "being chased and attacked" (56 percent). Other common themes reported by the survey were sexual experiences (54 percent), accomplishing something great (52 percent), flying or floating under one's own power (45 percent), paralysis or being unable to run or scream (42 percent … this one makes a lot of sense given our physical paralysis in REM sleep), taking exams (31 percent), missing a plane or train (28 percent), and being naked in public (15 percent).

Naturally, even the negative dream themes may not always be nightmarish, even if there may be sensations of frustration accompanying a dream with such an occurrence. While the falling dreams may be most common in this survey, not everyone who has a falling dream may consider it a nightmare. The type of dream most often considered the common nightmare is that of being chased or attacked, and you often hear people talk about the nightmare they had of someone dying, or the one where they were in front of a group about to act or speak and suddenly noticed that they were stark naked, or the nightmare where you are in a crowd and can't get anyone to notice you. All of these betray feelings of vulnerability, of helplessness, and of anxieties about not meeting our own expectations (or the expectations of others).

A 2006 survey in the United Kingdom by the hotel company Travelodge points to one in five people having a "bad dream" at least once a week, with 3 percent of all respondents having a nightmare every night. That survey, and others, added additional dream themes such as teeth falling out, dreams with animals and insects, taking an exam, and celebrity-laden dreams.

Other relatively recent surveys have been done cross-culturally, with different lists of the top ten most frequent themes in dreams. For example, a 2008 survey of Chinese students indicated the top two most common themes were school-related and being chased, echoing a 2004 survey of German students. However, a 2003 survey of Canadian students put being chased as number one and sexual experience dreams second.

According to one leading researcher of nightmares, Dr. Ernest Hartmann, there are two types of nightmares. There is a *standard* nightmare, which is like any other dream, though with the additional label of "nightmare" because of its content. There are also *post-traumatic* nightmares, a result of the experience of real events in one's life that may be stressful, scary, and even terrifying. Such events as being in an accident, an earthquake or some other disaster, or a soldier or law enforcement officer who is a participant in a violent scene may cause post-traumatic stress syndrome, which can often have long-term effects. Post-traumatic stress syndrome is being addressed by psychotherapists as a cause of continuing psychological and emotional adjustment problems as people try to relate to their normal lives after experiencing something unsettling or horrible.

The post-traumatic nightmares are often a result of living through disasters or being witnesses to or victims of accidents or personal attacks. Such nightmares are often replays of the actual events, causing people to relive horrible, true experiences, rather than being related to other forms of fantasy-dream imagery. For example, I've spoken with people in the San Francisco Bay area who had nightmares for weeks related to their experience of the October 17, 1989, earthquake.

In July 1993, I was at work on the twenty-fifth floor of 101 California Street in San Francisco when a gunman came in and opened fire in a law firm on the thirty-fourth floor—a law firm that was a client of my employer, LexisNexis. The gunman's spree continued on several floors and the building went on lockdown. Things were more than a bit tense with my fellow employees as we learned what was going on. Police came to all offices until and even after the gunman was found dead (he shot himself, eventually), checking everyone in case he had accomplices in the building (he did not). We all knew at least a couple of the people who were killed. Over the next week or two, I spoke with several people who worked in the building who were having nightmares because of the events, even those who were not witness to any of the sights or sounds of the actual shooting.

Veterans of Vietnam and other wars, as well as police officers involved in shoot-outs, who have experienced situations where people die in front of them or where they (the dreamers) caused those people's deaths (whether justifiably defending themselves or not) may relive the experiences. In addition, such traumatic experiences may even show up in waking experience, as "daymares" (more on this in the last section of this chapter).

Such trauma-related nightmares were also reported by many after the 9/11 attack, and examples are easily found with a simple Google search. There were also a number of people who reported having prophetic dreams of the attack, some with greater detail and others just an emotion-filled dream, who also continued having nightmares after.

Disaster Dreams Impact Us

In looking at psychic experience in dreams, there are numerous reports of both precognitive and clairvoyant dreams of disasters that may affect the dreamer emotionally. If I somehow psychically pick up on the death and devastation caused by a major earthquake or terrorist attack, I may react to that information in my dreams as though I had actually witnessed it. Since psychic perceptions tend to be very emotionally charged, one may receive precognitive/clairvoyant messages from both those who have been injured in the disaster as well as from the witnesses who look on in horror.

Unfortunately, the person experiencing such a psychic flow may actually have a recurring nightmare of the event, a form of psychically induced post-traumatic nightmare. There appears to be less of an emotional attachment to the nightmare if it's recognized as a psychic dream, and it's likely that, on some level of awareness, there is that kind of recognition (that this is not a normal dream) and the nightmare will not reoccur. On the other hand, if the dreamer feels that what was experienced was a clear, precognitive dream, there may be an overwhelming sense that he/she should try to do something about the dreamed-about situation (warn people at least). In chapter 10, I'll discuss the issue of acting on such premonitions.

Such psychic dreams of disaster that may reoccur also may not be very clear. I've spoken with more than a few people, including a few psychics, who had non-specific dreams about the 1989 San Francisco quake. Only two people I've spoken with claimed to have had a vivid dream of the quake and its effect on the Bay area, and neither of them consider themselves psychic. The psychics I've spoken with reported a general feeling of dread that something bad was going to happen in the area, but no specifics. And most of them reported the sensation building in them or the dreams occurring within forty-eight hours before the quake. This may not be related to precognitive experience, but to a sensitivity to the geomagnetic field of the earth, or some other such physical variables that relate to earthquakes.

However, unrelated to the geomagnetic field would be similar experiences of people before the 9/11 attack. Whether in dreams or while awake, a number of us who were members of a listserv for intuitives and researchers at the time expressed a general feeling of dread and foreboding the night before the attack, with some claiming that they woke up with that feeling, even though they could not recall the specific content of their dream. In my own case, the best way I can explain my feeling of dread was that there was "a disturbance in the Force" that kept me wide awake until hours after midnight, and something in a dream woke me up suddenly at the same time the first plane was hitting the tower.

In dealing with post-traumatic nightmares, feelings of guilt and helplessness may accompany the dreams. The best way to deal with such nightmares appears to be to talk about the nightmare and the events that the nightmare represents. Working through the feelings brought on by the original event appears to best alleviate trauma related to experiencing that event, whether the feelings keep coming back in nightmares or not.

The Standard Nightmare

Again, standard nightmares are dreams that go a bit further from any feeling of normal frustration or guilt or slight bits of fear. They are extreme in presenting the imagery in ways that induce negative emotional reactions that may spill over to our waking consciousness. Anxiety in nightmares may reflect some situation we saw as a failure in our waking lives, or may simply relate to not being able to function normally in our dreams, a sense of helplessness as the dream proceeds around us. Nightmares may reflect reactions to real events, essentially representations of anxiety or fear surrounding dealing with those events (divorce and other relationship issues, work problems, health problems, death in the family, accidents, and so on) where we feel that normal means of dealing with those situations are not effective.

Nightmares may be triggered by such stressful or traumatic situations as mentioned above or by any situation that may remind us of feelings of vulnerability or helplessness, such as what we felt when we were children. Nightmares may sometimes last longer than other dreams, as though the emotion carried by the dream takes time to build. Of course, what also appears to happen is that as the emotions build, we may react to them in that nightmare and wake up. If the nightmare brings on an intense reaction quickly, it will generally be a shorter dream.

The content of nightmares may relate to our waking state as much as any other dream. Our moods just before going to sleep do affect our dreams, and therefore may cause a dream to be viewed as a nightmare. Scary movies or books may make us feel uneasy enough that it's not only tough to go to sleep but we end up with some of that scary imagery in our dreams. This is especially true with children, according to a recent study.

Nightmares may be excellent indicators of problems we're facing in our lives. Looking at what goes on in a nightmare as an indication of an unresolved issue or as some way of telling ourselves that there's something wrong here may yield much information about ourselves. Nightmares may be warnings to the conscious mind by another part of ourselves, integrating information about ourselves or about situations in our waking lives, the outer world, that we're not consciously aware of. As all the information that comes through our senses is processed, there may be items that we miss on the conscious level, which we are made aware of through dreams and nightmares. Recurring nightmares can tell us as much about an issue that needs addressing as can any other recurring dream—it's recurring because we're not dealing with it, whatever *it* turns out to be.

To bring it back to the psychic side of things, nightmares can be actual warnings of dangerous situations or individuals that will affect us or others. The key is to face the information in that nightmare and ask yourself "Why is that there? What can it be saying to me … or about me?"

Dealing with Nightmares

There are many views on dealing with nightmares. Dr. Ernest Hartmann, author of *The Nightmare: The Psychology and Biology of Terrifying Dreams,* has written that we can avoid nightmares by figuring out what it is in our life that makes us afraid or feel helpless. Some awareness of what really frustrates us or stresses us out may help us recognize the nightmare imagery for what it is more easily. Dr. Stephen LaBerge and many others suggest facing up to that nightmare monster in the dream. Either through the use of lucid dreaming or that by programming yourself with the idea that you will turn and face whatever is bad in that nightmare, you may be able to confront the nightmare image and overcome it, absorb it, or get information that may shed light over what it represents.

"Why are you here? What do you represent? What do I need to be aware of in myself to change the outcome of the event represented by this image that frightens me?" Turning in the nightmare and facing up to your fears, rather than running from them as we normally do in nightmares, may in itself be enough to alleviate the point of the nightmare, to allow you to recognize the image for what it really represents. Asking the above questions may take you a bit further in dealing with the issues in your waking life. It appears that facing up to these nightmares makes the most awful issues easy to deal with, and helps make sure they don't reoccur. Remember, it's typically the unresolved issues that cause recurrent nightmares.

You must acknowledge the nightmare images in order to deal with them. Some experts feel that to ignore or avoid these images that are trying to tell you something may send those feelings or other source issues deeper into your unconscious, to later reappear (possibly even stronger). Acknowledging the images, no matter how fearful they seem to be, as part of yourself, realizing that the monster you see in the nightmare is part of you, conjured up by you to tell you something, can often be enough to end the nightmare. The belief that the image "has no power over me," whether occurring in a lucid dream where you are aware you're in a nightmare or whether you simply believe that in your waking state, helps you overcome and work through the nightmares.

Facing up to the image may be the best way to go while in a lucid dream. Reactions in lucid dreams to nightmarish imagery may involve actively changing the dream to remove whatever that bad image is. In other words, if you are lucid in a nightmare, and aware that you have the power in that dream to change things, you may be tempted to simply whisk away the bad stuff and replace it with something else, or simply remove yourself from the scene, escaping in effect. According to Dr. Gayle Delaney, that might not always be the best way to go. This could cause the nightmare to reoccur simply because you are not dealing with or exploring what it is the images represent. The issues in the outer world, the waking world, that the images symbolize are not recognized or dealt with, and therefore the nightmares may continue.

Adults Having Nightmares

Before you get too involved in worrying about how you're going to deal with your next nightmare, keep in mind that most of us rarely have nightmares, unless we end up in a situation where post-traumatic stress syndrome could cause them (or you really are buying into the fear provided by many horror films … though that type of nightmare rarely reoccurs). What about those people (the 1 in 200 to 500) who have nightmares frequently?

Dr. Ernest Hartmann has studied the types of people in this group, the frequent nightmare sufferers, and come to some conclusions. Hartmann talks in terms of people having boundaries between being awake and dreaming, and between reality and fantasy. People with *thin boundaries* between these states are most prone to nightmares in adulthood. They are people who are usually very sensitive (possibly hypersensitive) and trusting (sometimes overly so). There is often some ambiguity with regards to sexual identity, not being either strongly masculine or feminine, often recognizing both sides of themselves (though not necessarily or even generally homosexual or even bisexual). They may be prone to daydreaming. Many nightmare sufferers have difficulty waking up or gaining certainty that they are really awake (and not still asleep and dreaming).

And, interestingly enough, they are often people with very creative inclinations toward art, music, writing, and other such endeavors. Besides Robert Louis Stevenson, who had a nightmare that brought him *Dr. Jekyll and Mr. Hyde*, Mary Wollstonecraft Shelley wrote *Frankenstein* as a result of a nightmare.

Creative people tend not to be rigid in their thinking patterns, often looking at the world around them in a number of ways to get different viewpoints. An ability to fantasize, to merge reality and fantasy, obviously helps the creative person, and may allow for more non-realistic imagery to come through in dreams.

As we grow up, most of us learn to not only differentiate between what is reality and what is fantasy, but to build boundaries for ourselves separating the two. This not only helps us from mixing up the two (fantasy and reality) on a conscious level, it also helps protect us from potentially damaging or frightening information that might keep pouring into our dreams and conscious awareness. People with thin boundaries may not have such well-developed defense mechanisms, and therefore may end up with a spill-over of fantasy imagery in dreams and nightmares, as well as in daydreams.

Daydreams

Daydreaming, fantasizing while awake, is a natural state for many people. Our minds tend to wander a bit into our own memories every day, and may purposefully seek out certain images because what is in front of us in reality is pretty dull and boring. Daydreams tend to involve a replay of events, perhaps with slightly different outcomes, or may be a practice for an event about to happen (like asking someone out on a date or asking the boss for a raise). Daydreams tend to involve some emotion as well.

Most daydreams happen spontaneously and are close to, if not exactly about, everyday events. People can, however, be deliberate about their daydreams, causing them to run a certain course beyond their own lives (putting themselves "in other people's shoes," so to speak) or even leap beyond the bounds of reality as we know it. As a science fiction and comic books reader, I realize there has to be a certain amount of structure within someone's imaginings to create the stories in the books I've read. Writing about fictional characters at all involves a bit of daydreaming as you try to project the story in your mind and get it down in your computer or on paper.

Daydreaming can even be encouraged and guided by outside forces. Guided visualization, where another person (or audio recording of another person) suggests a certain course for your daydream, can be of great benefit. Besides being a way to exercise the imagination, guided visualizations have been helpful in uncovering emotional problems and in doing a bit of self-healing; they are often quite beneficial to people. You can consider such outer-caused daydreams as a form of meditation.

Daymares

Unfortunately, with the good comes the bad, in this case in the form of a *daymare*—daydreams of disaster, of death, of accidents, or of other negative outcomes of events that could adversely affect you and others. People do have daymares caused by fears and worries ("what if my wife is cheating on me?" or "what if this plane I'm about to board blows an engine?"), and they can be quite similar to nightmares we have while asleep. Daymares may be replays of tragic events witnessed or participated in, and may be caused by post-traumatic stress syndrome or simply by watching the evening news and worrying about what you see (which is often negative, violent imagery). They can result from stress at work or by socially emphasized problems (such as AIDS or the threat of a terrorist attack).

The differences between daymares and nightmares are often quite pronounced, as are similarities between the two. The same issues and experiences that cause nightmares may result in daymares. The differences, however, are important. With a nightmare, you are asleep, and unless you're in a lucid dream, have little conscious control over what goes on. With a daymare, you are awake, capable of consciously recognizing what's there, and capable of consciously ending the scenario, or of being distracted by other people or outside happenings (thereby ending the daymare). And the daymares relate more closely to virtual reality than do the fantastic images that may appear in a nightmare. (Although it may be quite unrealistic for many to daydream that your spouse is cheating on you, that's more realistic than dreaming your spouse has become a fifty-foot-tall monster, isn't it?)

Fantasy-prone individuals may, of course, include quite unrealistic imagery in their daydreams and therefore in their daymares (do horror fiction writers have daymares or do they simply daydream since their own imagery doesn't generally frighten them?).

What About Psi?

Psi ties in here in a couple of ways.

There have been studies of what personality characteristics are included in people who are more psychic than others. One of those is creativity. In studies with artists, writers, and musicians as compared to control groups not in the creative arts, the creative types came out ahead, often significantly so, in results indicating psi ability in the tests. Creative types appear to be more psychic, yet that may be simply because they tend not to view the world in absolutes, but more in possibilities than others—though I know plenty of individuals who cross that line. They may be more open to psi or belief in psi, and therefore allow the experiences and information to flow rather than dismissing it as not real or blocking it out altogether.

Psi experiences occur not only in dreams and nightmares, but also in daydreams and daymares. In fact, you might have a psychic experience with vivid imagery or information presented to you while awake and dismiss it as a daydream, or there may be a sudden flash of a disaster occurring that you shake off as imagination (albeit negative).

How do you tell the difference? As you will see as you read on in this book, the difference tends to be in the quality of the experience—you just *know*. Whether you act on that information, or even *can* act on it at all flows from whether you can even recognize the information as real and not imagined. Unfortunately, this is not easy to do, especially when the information comes through while we are daydreaming; it seems easier to rationalize it away.

Dying in Your Dreams

One other question comes up with regards to nightmares. As mentioned, the original thought surrounding nightmares had to do with evil spirits invading our dreams, with probable intentions to do us harm. The plot of the movie *Inception* is predicated on individuals being able to enter and affect the dreams of others. The entire *Nightmare on Elm Street* series has to do with the spirit of Freddy Kruger invading the dreams of the living and, basically, hurting or killing them in reality by affecting them in their dreams.

What happens if you die in your dream or nightmare? From personal experience, I can say I have died in a couple of dreams and I'm still around. I did not, fortunately or unfortunately, continue on in my dream to an afterlife, although I remember one dream from college days where I dreamed of dying and haunting my roommates (it was fun!). I've spoken to others who have also experienced death in their dreams, and I've continued that falling dream, as have others, until I actually hit the ground. Usually, I just got up and brushed myself off, having no damage to my (dream) body at all (eat your heart out, Wile E. Coyote!). Of course, I was a fan of Looney Toons growing up.

Do people die as a result of their nightmares? Probably not. The *probably* is only because if people really have died as a result of a nightmare, we have no information that the dream was the cause of death, no way of knowing since there's no one around to tell us. No ghosts, to my knowledge, have shown up claiming this to be the way they died. So, since many have reported dying in dreams and lived to tell about it, we can probably assume there's nothing to worry about.

We have much to learn from nightmares (and even day-mares) as they truly betray what is bothering us, what our deep-seated fears and anxieties are, and what the unresolved issues are in our lives. Looking at nightmares as helpful tools, as indicators of those unresolved issues, may make them easier to live with.

Then again, maybe you can use that nightmare to become the next Stephen King or Dean Koontz...

chapter 4
The Basis of Dreamwork:
Other Lands, Other Times, Other Dreams

We generally think of analyzing and working with dreams to be a fairly recent activity in human history, maybe only as recent as Freud's dream theories. But the working with dreams, the analysis and application of them, the programming of them, the fascination (or fear) with dreams, has been with humanity since the beginning. In fact, the observance of dreams and what they tell us may be the most prevalent form of divination, of obtaining advice from other sources with regards to past, present, and most importantly future, going back thousands of years.

The content and form of dreams of people from other cultures may vary as much as the cultural and mythic images of that group varies from those of other cultures. But the themes, the way we deal with them, are often the same. It's the same story, but the story is retold with different dressing, with appropriate cultural artifacts and labels, or from differing viewpoints. Dreams have always held information for us and have shaped our development, regardless of cultural background and beliefs. This points out that we are alike not only in our waking lives, but in our dreams as well. It's merely the window dressing of culture and religion that seems to separate us and our interpretations.

Sleep, Dreaming, Death, and the Divine

One of the oldest ideas about sleep and dreaming confuses sleep as some state related to death. The reduction of bodily function, the inability to move (especially during REM sleep), and the occasional dream remembrances of the sleeper all pointed to the concept that the spirit—the soul—of the sleeper actually left the body, as it does in death, though unlike death, the soul is called back to the body, returning life as the sleeper wakes. As in true death of the body, the life of the spirit continues after the body dies in sleep. Unlike death, sleep is only a temporary state, a respite for the soul so that it may wander the earth and other places unencumbered by the constraints of the flesh.

Along with this concept, some people see the dream state as one in which humanity can be in touch with divine entities, with the gods themselves, with wise beings (such as the spirits of our ancestors, or with some inspired part of our inner selves). The myths of people all over the world have connections to dreams, and dreams may reflect the mythology of the people, and therefore important societal, cultural, and very human issues, problems, and solutions.

According to mythologist Joseph Campbell in his book *The Hero with a Thousand Faces* (page 19): "Dream is the personalized myth, myth the depersonalized dream; both myth and dream are symbolic in the same general way of the dynamics of the psyche. But in the dream the forms are quirked by the peculiar troubles of the dreamer, whereas in myth the problems and solutions shown are directly valid for all mankind." He further goes on to say (page 101), "In our dreams, the ageless perils, gargoyles, trials, secret helpers, and instructive figures are nightly still encountered; and in their forms we may see reflected not only the whole picture of our present case, but also the clue to what we must do to be saved." Myths and dreams both are carriers of cultural metaphors.

Dreams and Ancient History

Our ancestors all over the world made much of the content of dreams, whether one considers their impact on forming a view of the world and its creation, or looking at those dreams as contacts with the supernatural, with the afterlife, and with the divine, or as omens of the future.

The study and analysis of dreams was an established cultural practice in ancient Mesopotamia, and dream analysis books have been found and decoded. However, dreams normally would be considered nothing more than omens, unless interpreted by experts, who might prescribe rituals to carry out or prevent what the dream was to have predicted. There were several types of dreams considered by the dream interpreters, including dreams of a prophetic nature, those carrying messages from the gods to kings or other important societal persons, and those which relate specifically to the dreamer, whether relating to health or to the personal future of the person having the dream. The Babylonians, often concerned with their future, used dreams as omens for the path of their waking lives.

The dream connections between royalty and the gods were also evident in the culture of the Egyptian pharaohs. The gods often appeared to the royalty with messages and advice to consider and carry out, or so they were interpreted. Because others besides royalty had dreams, and those dreams could not be messages from divine sources (who only spoke to royalty), a different form of dream interpretation and divination came about. The belief developed that one could ask for dreams that might provide answers or advice for the dreamer. At the same time, the ancient Hebrews saw dreams as connections between God and selected individuals charged with delivering God's word.

The ancient Greeks had a long tradition of working with dreams, although the ideas surrounding the source of dreams, how they could be used, and where the information in dreams came from changed over time. Dreams began as signs and messages from the gods, providing useful information to guide the dreamers' lives, or providing special peeks at the lives of the gods themselves. Later, health issues became the central points of the analysis and decoding of dreams, with people often obtaining the information through dream incubation practices.

Plato was interested in the ways dreams affected people's lives, though it was Aristotle who pushed the idea that dreams came from within the dreamer's experience, not from outside divine or other supernatural sources. Many interpreters of dreams dealt with specific kinds of dreams, applying the special information to anything from divination to healing. Hippocrates was one such healer who, when dealing with dreams at all, dealt only with those that had to do with the state of the body.

The most comprehensive written work from the Greeks comes from Artemidorus, in the second century AD, who wrote a volume called the *Oneirokritika,* considered by some the most comprehensive work before Freud. This book laid out a systematic way of dealing with dreams as an extension of daily life. He placed dreams in two major categories: those that were related to some event that was fairly immediate in time to the dreamer's experience, and those that were more symbolic or metaphorical and may have required more time to relate to the waking experience of the dreamer, with special regard to the individual characteristics of the dreamer.

Early Christians saw dreams as a time when the body and spirit were vulnerable to influences from the outside. Nightmares, of course, were those dreams in which demons and monsters, often sexually related demons (incubi and succubi), invaded or affected the body and soul of the dreamer in some way. Practices to deal with demons evolved in the religious context, as with other cultures. In examining other cultures with similar views of evil spirits attacking in the night, one often finds shamans, priests, medicine men, or others with rituals that help ward off outside supernatural influences. In such a view of dreams, it would be unlikely for people to want to open themselves to dreaming.

Asking for Messages: Dream Incubation

The practice of asking for something through dreams has always been very prevalent, since many consider dreaming as a time when we are open to outside influences (such as from the gods or ancestor spirits or even demons). In some cultures, dreams may not only present direct messages, but might be signals of power being achieved by the dreamer. Dream content may have in it lucky or unlucky omens, totems, and symbols, and purposefully dreaming of certain things may speak of the dreamer's own power, as with the Washoe Native American tribe of central California and Nevada. Asking for divine guidance or even achieving it with no direct request is part of many cultures. Much of the Koran was dictated to Muhammad in dreams, and there are other similar stories of important religious literature or lore passed on through dreams from apparently divine sources.

The practice of dream incubation for the programming of dreams can be connected with ancient cultures, from the Egyptians, Babylonians, and Phoenicians to ancient Hebrews and Greeks. In addition, it is a practice that was common among tribes of Native Americans, by peoples in the Himalayas, in China, in Japan, and in other places around the world.

In this practice, dreams are asked for and obtained by having the dreamer sleep at a particular sacred or magical site, such as a temple or a natural landmark associated with some divine power. There may be a ritual associated with the visit to the shrine, in asking for the powers-that-be to answer a problem with a visit of information (or the gods themselves) in the dream. The typical dream incubations began (more or less as cultural practice) as requests for prophecy or for spiritual insight, but became in Egyptian and Greek cultures, for example, requests for information with regards to personal health and well-being. The dreamers visited, possibly participated in a special ritual, and slept in (or near) the sacred place or object; in return they would have (and hopefully remember) a dream or dreams in which their questions and problems were addressed.

Dream Inducement

Another way to receive such information and advice comes in the form of dreams that are deliberately induced. Many peoples around the world have had some form of dream inducement included in rites of passage or in prayer for divine guidance. Such rituals may include the use of fasting, prayer, magical rituals, dancing, and even drugs, or some combination of these. Native

Americans, in particular, made use of (and still make use of) various methods of dream inducement in order to receive guidance or to become adults. The Ojibwa, for example, used fasting as a means for adolescent males to gain power, good fortune, and knowledge, revealed to them in dreams. The adult Native Americans of the plains sought the knowledge the soul could gather through their vision quests, which involved not only fasting, but sometimes self-torture or mutilation. Whether such visions occurred during sleep or not is difficult to say (except perhaps on a case-by-case basis), but the importance of the dream/visions was evident in their cultures.

Drug-induced dreams and dream ceremonies occur in cultures all over the world, whether through the ingesting of sacred mushrooms or some other fungus or through the taking into the body of other natural substances such as hallucinogens that create other bodily reactions. The difficulty in looking at such practices, however, is in dealing with when the dream happens. Such substances may place the individual in an altered state of consciousness while still awake or may influence the dreams of that individual once he or she has gone to sleep.

Other forms of programming dreams also occur, including the idea of working with requests in lucid dreaming or simply focusing on a request or subject matter before going to sleep, with the hopes (often justified) that our own minds will address such things in dreams.

Native American Dreams

The importance of dreams in other cultures is part of the historical and anthropological record. Other tribes such as the Winnebago and Algonquin had their adolescents search out dream visions as part of their rites of passage. The Mohave see dreams as a source of knowledge about workings of their societies and religion, though often presented in mythic form, and therefore needing interpretation (by shamans) to be accepted as true. The Navajo medicine men spend their first waking moments in the morning contemplating and interpreting their dreams, and often deciding whether there are events in the dreams that need to be dealt with in the waking world, either symbolically or ritualistically.

The Iroquois nations dealt with dreams extensively. In reports from missionaries during the seventeenth century, it was seen that the Seneca and Huron nations of the Iroquois had their own ways of dealing with their dreams (which were heavily invested with power), ways that could be called psychoanalytic by today's standards. They saw dreams as manifesting secret wishes of the soul and portraying them through dreams and as vehicles for supernatural beings to relay messages and wishes for the dreamer or for the entire community.

The Iroquois recognized the importance of dream symbology and what it had to say to the individual and the community as a whole. They recognized that the interpretation could sometimes be the opposite of what the dream said, and they therefore often needed interpretation by someone other than the dreamer. In order to relieve any stress indicated by the symbology of the dreams, dreamers acted out the situations in their dreams, though often in a symbolic way. In doing so, by effectively carrying out the dream scenarios in some symbolic, ritualistic, or real way, they were essentially dealing with the frustrated desires presented by the dreams. The sharing of dreams was essential to this process.

On the other side of the coin are the Maricopa of Colorado. As with other peoples, they believed that while dreaming the spirit or soul leaves the body. The spirit seeks out another spirit or supernatural being who will eventually lead them down the path of knowledge, through success in a spiritual journey (which would lead to success in life). This was a long process for them, and speaking of such dreams depended on how far along one was on that journey. Speaking of the dreams too soon could cause the other spirit—the guardian of the dream journey—to abandon the dreamer.

More cultures seem to be of the Iroquois mind on the issue of discussing dreams. The Chippewa actively cultivated dreaming as a means for receiving knowledge about themselves and the world around them. Children were encouraged to try to remember their dreams, and the male rite of passage also included a fasting ritual in order to receive the important dream vision.

Senoi Dreamwork

Probably the most frequently mentioned culture that deals directly with dreams is the Senoi of Malaysia. The late Kilton Stewart was the first to write about the "dreaming people" as they are often called, having visited them and studied their culture back in the mid-1930s. According to Stewart, the Senoi are a particularly cooperative and peaceful people, with little or no crime or conflict and very few mental health problems. Whether the lack of violence and the presence of such a cooperative spirit actually is a result of their daily dreamwork (as postulated by Stewart and others) is unproven. However, their unique views on resolving conflict through one's dreams has been adopted by many therapists and dreamworkers.

The Senoi believed that each person has his or her own internal universe and forces to deal with that connect with the outside world, and that they should learn to master these internal forces from childhood. Patricia Garfield, PhD, in her book *Creative Dreaming*, relates three steps the Senoi take toward that mastery of conflict presented in dreams or present in their waking lives. Dreamers are to "confront and conquer dream danger," "advance toward dream pleasure," and "achieve a positive outcome." To do this, they learned to program their dreams, to shape them by suggestion, and often to work in a lucid dreaming state.

Their activities in the social context often center around the sharing of dreams, starting with sharing and discussion of dreams at breakfast with one's family. Later in the day, individuals might continue this process with friends or colleagues.

Dealing with any conflict presented in the dreams might come through direct play within the dreams, acting out and working through problems in the dreams, or through acting out (in the waking world) what was presented in the dream, whether realistically, symbolically, or ritualistically. Programming or working with the dream is the most common method of working through situations. They might recreate a situation from their daily lives in a dream in order to deal with that problem, or they may confront a problem presented first in a dream (unrecognized or even nonexistent in real life). Dreamers must confront ideas and characters present in their dreams, calling on friends or other helpers necessary to deal with the dream situation. Dream characters are only harmful, bad, as long as the dreamer is afraid and retreats from them. Facing them and winning a battle or a conflict in a dream often results in the bad character becoming good. Altering your own actions within the dream also helps. For example, purposefully causing the flying dream to continue, though changing the falling into flying under your own (dream) power empowers you, the dreamer.

I should mention that there has been criticism of the Senoi dream theory that attempts to minimize the importance of dreams to the tribes at the time Stewart did his work with them. But we can really only look at what was written about them with an eye toward the question of "But does it work?" The answer to that has been a resounding "Yes."

Aboriginal Dreaming: Not What We Expect

For the Australian Aborigines, there is the Dreaming (with a capital D), also called the Dream Time. The Dreaming is time everlasting, an eternal Now from which everything else has sprung. The world we live in sprang from the Dreaming ages ago, on the say-so of various deities that live in that reality, which is more real than our own. While the reference to the time of the Dreaming typically refers to a creative era, to that time long ago when our world came out of it, Aborigines use the term to refer also to the present and future, as that past from which we sprung continues to be relevant to our world and all things (and people) living on it.

Looking to the Dreaming, to the Dream Time, for information, for inspiration, and for action is part of the Aborigine culture, and reinforces their cultural belief in the connections of humans and the natural world. The Dreaming yields information that we might consider psychic, and there have been reports of Aborigines using their connection to the Dreaming to enable them to do things we might consider unusual, if not paranormal.

Dreams (with a small d) do play a role in connecting with the Dreaming, though dreams are by no means more than one small way to connect with this other reality. According to Ronald Rose in his study of the psychic life of Aborigines *(Living Magic,* page 141): " ... as with us, clear-cut, vivid dreams, dreams that are easily remembered, comparatively free from distortion, rich in detail, are those to which Aborigines attach considerable importance."

There is an Aboriginal belief that holds man as a reincarnation of a being from the Dreaming. Before the birth of a child, a totem creature from the Dreaming makes itself known to one or both parents or to other close relatives in a dream. That dream of such a spiritual being connects the baby to the Dreaming, to the baby's preexistent form in the Dreaming. With that link, a bit of the totem's power is passed. The dream seems to be a necessary medium in establishing that link to the Dreaming. In essence, one might look at dreams in such a context as establishing the reality of the newborn, since the physical reality in which we're born into is an extension of the reality of the Dream Time.

Dream or Reality?

Other cultures tell us that working with dreams can help us in our spiritual journeys through life as well as in dealing with reality. The question of reality and what is real is an important one, especially in connection to dreaming. Do we know, at any given point, that we are not dreaming, that we are really awake? Pinching yourself may not help, as you could dream of pinching yourself and feeling pain. Ever had a dream of waking up and turning off the alarm clock, only to have that turn out to be a dream (and you know this only because you wake up and turn off the alarm a *second* time)?

Stephen LaBerge suggests trying something that shouldn't work in real life, such as flying or floating under your own power. I suggest a simple levitation or flight around the room, not a leap off (or over) a tall building (which, I'm sure, is not something Dr. LaBerge would suggest either). If you fly, you're probably dreaming (or you ought to be wearing a costume and a cape).

This question of reality and dreaming is an important one to some cultures. There are people around the world who believe (as a culture) that what happens in a dream is real. Some believe that the soul or spirit actually does leave the body and can travel around this world (or other dimensions) and even observe real situations, bringing back information. This kind of dream belief would be considered by many to be indicative of out-of-body experiences.

Others, such as the Ashanti in Africa and the Kai in New Guinea, believe that what happens in a dream *is* reality. If you dreamed of traveling to Japan, you really did, according to such a belief system. And there is the belief of other peoples that what occurs in a dream is reality, but not necessarily the reality we live in.

The issue of reality and what it is, in and out of dreams, is a question being approached by many fields, from philosophy to quantum physics. Dreams present an interesting paradox, in that we rely on our subjective experiences to tell if we are dreaming or not. More than 1,500 years ago, the Chinese philosopher Chuang Tzu explained the paradox of subjective experience and dreams: "One night, I dreamed I was a butterfly, fluttering here and there, content with my lot. Suddenly I awoke and I was Chuang Tzu again. Who am I in reality? A butterfly dreaming that I am Chuang Tzu, or Chuang Tzu dreaming he was a butterfly?"

Another way I've heard that expressed is as a question: "Are we real or are we characters in the dream of God or some other being? And what happens if he (or she) wakes up?"

We'll have to assume we are real, at least until you finish reading this book. The question of "What is reality?" is a subject for other books and discussions, since it seems to be a lot easier to tell if we are dreaming, as suggested by Stephen LaBerge, than deciding what reality is.

Believing that messages from dreams hold information from beyond ourselves leaves us with possible spiritual connections, to psychic realms beyond our own. It is on the psychic level that we connect, that we become more like one another.

chapter 5
Conscious While Dreaming: Lucid Dreams

A friend or loved one presents you with an interesting proposal for a weekend trip. Needing to take a day or two off from work to go on this trip, you say, "Let me go home and sleep on it." That night you sleep and begin to dream.

In the dream, you suddenly realize you're completely aware you are in a dream. In the dreamworld, you can explore the possible benefits and consequences of the trip and taking the time off from work. You go through the possibilities, come to a decision, and remind yourself to remember the dream when you wake up. That day, you call your friend and pass on your decision, feeling good because you literally "slept on it."

Conscious, aware it *is* a *dream*?

This is lucid dreaming, a particular kind of dream state for which we have evidence in the historical record going back as far as we have records of dreams themselves. While the lucid dream is not one everyone experiences, according to many experts it is one everyone can ease into or learn, and it is a particular dream state that has only gained acceptance in the last quarter of the twentieth century.

The Rough Path to Acceptance
Starts with Psychical Research

The term *lucid* as applied to dreams is credited to the Dutch physician Frederik Willems Van Eeden in 1913, who coined and presented it in a paper to the British Society for Psychical Research (SPR), the world's oldest formal society studying psychic phenomena from a scientific standpoint. However, while the term and recognition of the state of lucidity goes back to 1913, and the historical record of such experiences much further, lucid dreaming has had to travel a rocky road to acceptance.

After Van Eeden, British parapsychologist Celia Green was the first to extensively discuss the dream state in her book *Lucid Dreams* in the 1960s. A scholarly work, it unfortunately did nothing for the acceptance of lucid dreams as a real dream experience. It was perhaps the association of lucid dreams to psychic phenomena that created such acceptance problems.

Psychic experience and parapsychology have for a long time faced acceptance problems, with a great deal of denial by the scientific mainstream. Even though lucidity in dreams is not a psychic phenomenon, that the lucid dream got its label in a paper to the SPR and the first scholarly treatment in a book by a parapsychologist did nothing to interest the psychological community that was ignoring and often lambasting anything to do with parapsychology, psychic phenomena, or the popular occult.

While Green's work saw little acceptance, there was a growing interest in the sixties to look at altered states of consciousness. Dr. Charles Tart's work with altered states did much for the interest in them and, by association, the interest in dream states.

(Tart is perhaps best known to others with respect to his work in parapsychology—there's that connection again.)

The writings of Patricia Garfield, PhD, a San Francisco therapist (see her book *Creative Dreaming),* and Ann Faraday, PhD, (*Dream Power, The Dream Game*) in the seventies worked wonders with introducing many concepts having to do with dreamwork and lucid dreams into the general public's consciousness. The writings of Carlos Castaneda have also been credited as having a great impact on awareness of altered states, dreaming, and lucid dreaming.

However, it is the experimental work on lucidity in dreams at Stanford University by Stephen LaBerge and others in the late seventies that finally brought the beginnings of acceptance. The early work at Stanford on lucid dreams came from the angle of communication from the dream state. If you were aware and conscious in the dream state, and the rapid eye movements could be correlated to particular movements of the dreamer within the dream, a code of sorts could be worked out and communication could take place. LaBerge, himself skilled at lucid dreaming, and others so skilled (whom he has called *oneironauts*) were able to communicate from within their dream states, thus showing that such a conscious dream state does exist.

It's interesting to note that while the folks at Stanford were working on their lucid dream studies in the late seventies, Keith Hearne at the University of Hull in England was working with lucid dreamer Alan Worsley, also using eye movements as communication from the lucid dream state. While Hearne published first, it is to the group at Stanford that credit for gaining acceptance of lucid dreaming goes to.

Eye Movement Correlations

Particular patterns of eye movements were agreed upon and carried out by the oneironauts, which led to other studies and findings, including the aforementioned correlation that elapsed time in the dream state is approximately the same as that in the world outside the dream. Part of the reason time compression may not be *able* to work relates to the time it takes the pathways of the brain to send signals and do anything with them. No matter how fast we think, we can't keep track of significantly small fragments of a second. For full months to actually occur as minutes, something would have to change in the speed at which we process that information. Hence the use of techniques similar to the movies or theater in compressing time, techniques which likely were inspired by dreams to begin with.

Studies of lucid dreams indicate that the imagery produced in such a dream can seem more real than what we see in the physical world. Colors are more vivid, everything is in sharper focus, and it seems ultra-real. Recognition of that, in itself, may be a way a person wakes up in the dream. Dream imagery is reported to be more like reality than any imagery we can produce in visualization practices while awake.

How Do We Become Lucid?

Generally this happens spontaneously, and people often remember such single-occurrence lucid dreams, though they appear to be infrequent or really one-time occurrences. Lucid dreaming on a more-than-once-in-a-great-while basis seems to be a natural occurrence in 5 to 10 percent of the population. Dr. Jayne Gackenbach and others have suggested that lucid dreamers are less likely to be neurotic or depressed personalities.

Most lucid dreams occur because something within the dream alerts the dreamer that it *is* a dream. Thoughts within the dream such as "Isn't this odd?" or "This can't really be happening, can it?" or a recognition that what's going on bears little resemblance to real experience can seemingly jog the consciousness of the dreamer to come to the conclusion of "Oh, I must be dreaming."

Memory or recognition of a situation being one we've experienced before can spark lucidity. For example, let's say you're having a dream of going on vacation. You board the plane, arrive at the destination, and suddenly realize you'd been there before with the same people; it's like a déjà vu experience in the dream. This may bring on a realization that it is, in fact, a memory, that some aspects of the experience seem too real or maybe unreal, and bring on a questioning of yourself about whether you're dreaming or not. Questioning the reality of the dream is a first step to lucidity in that dream, as it will put you toward some detachment within the dream, where you are now examining the reality in which you find yourself a bit more closely, looking for other signs that it is a dream.

To stay lucid in the dream, we apparently need some degree of detachment, as though we continue to remind our (dream) selves that we are dreaming, that what is being observed and participated in is just a dream. This self in the dream is a construct, whether it's you or some version of yourself you create or even another character role. Remembering that the "role" is just that so you don't get too involved in playing the part appears to be important. Forgetting it's a dream might end the lucidity of it.

If you feel yourself falling out of the lucid state within your dream, you might try to focus your (dream) attention on an object or an individual in the dream. Garfield suggests that a constant state of alertness in the lucid dream may be necessary to stay lucid, while "there is a danger that excitement over the joy of your freedom and power will wake you" (Garfield, *Creative Dreaming*, page 120). Somehow, you have to strike a happy medium. In addition, you can program yourself, while awake or while in the dream, to remember you are dreaming. "I will remember I'm dreaming" might be a good mantra to repeat before sleep or while in the dream. LaBerge has suggested that if you feel yourself falling out of lucidity, you spin your dream self around like a top or like a small child would. This spinning technique apparently keeps you on your own focused, conscious awareness of the dream.

Limits of What We Can Do

While we seem to be able to perform miracles in lucid dreams, there is some degree of equivalence to our actual physical selves as far as what we can do or accomplish in the dream state, as though there are still some limits on our own abilities. However, such limitations may be stronger with regard to mental achievements than physical ones. Controlling the dream (or your imagination) so you picture yourself as Superman knocking an asteroid off its collision course with Earth would be easier than, say, dreaming (or imagining) what it's like to be a super-genius.

There appears to be some internally consistent logic being applied, so that miracles are possible given the physical laws of the dreamworld you've created. Science fiction differs from fantasy fiction in that true science fiction is based on the laws of our universe and extrapolations from those laws. There is often a bending of such laws to allow for plot devices such as faster-than-light travel or time travel (which may not be impossible even by current laws of physics), and certainly extraterrestrial life is plausible. These are tales based on science. Fantasy, on the other hand, usually involves magic or supernatural forces that can play with the fabric of reality and supersede the laws of physics. Good fantasy fiction, however, also creates its own laws, so that even magic works according to the rules, which are usually logical when related to one another.

Our dreams, therefore, may create new rules to play by, but are still limited to internal logic and to what our imaginations can come up with. There are, however, limitations to other mental activities. For example, most lucid dreamers find reading very hard, if not impossible, to do. You might try reading as a test to see if you are dreaming or not. If you pick up a book and can read it, you are generally awake. If you can't read it, or you turn away and back and it now says something different (the text has changed), you are undoubtedly dreaming (and that realization may be enough to cause you to be completely lucid in the dream).

In discussing psychic abilities with psychics, and specifically with people who are good at remote viewing, it seems that reading is often difficult if not impossible when receiving information clairvoyantly. Visual images make much better targets for psychics, and one might make the analogy to the translation of verbal information (spoken or read while awake) into images while dreaming.

In general, our own actions in the dreams are similar to those in waking life. Since our own nondeliberate actions tend to follow along within certain boundaries in dreams, deliberate, conscious action applied within the lucid dream (when applied to using the dreams for problem-solving or some other applications) should bear some resemblance to reality. In confronting a problem situation, such as making a decision about going away for the weekend and having to miss a day of work, throwing in a magical or miraculous solution (such as, say, having someone in the dream hand you a check for a million dollars so you can quit your job, or stopping time in the dream so you can go without missing a day of work) will not help too much when applying the dream solutions to real-life conditions. And while destroying the evil ogre that is your boss may be cathartic in the dream and help you feel better, you certainly won't go far when faced with the real-life boss (not unless you know any magic sword dealers).

Working On Solutions

What good are lucid dreams if you can't play with reality in order to get to solutions? First of all, looking for solutions to real-life conflict in a lucid dream does not mean you can't be creative in how you play with the possible solutions. Running through a series of possible scenarios based on different decisions still allows a great deal of play with reality. By expressing some degree of control in your dream, the solution presented to any problem or issue is based on your ability to think through the problem and possible solutions, rather than on reflex action (as might be presented in a normal dream).

You can even look for creative solutions to physical problems or for ways to rehearse physical movements, as mentioned in the last chapter. As a magician and mentalist, I've learned several sleight-of-hand moves by rehearsing them over and over in my (waking) mind. Somehow, that has made performing the effect much easier even the first time, and made it look a lot better to my audience (since, mentally, I can view the effect as it is seen from the audience's perspective).

So, within the lucid dreamworld, you can take a better look at problems you're having and observe what the benefits or consequences of any chain of events you set into motion might be, almost as if you are both scriptwriter and director of the film that is your dream. At a moment's notice, you can change the script, add or subtract characters, and redirect the actions toward new conclusions. Engaging dream characters in conversation will enable the you that is creating the dream to interact with the you that is lucid in the dream.

As an aid to decision-making, the lucid dream can be invaluable in weighing all possibilities. You can be creative in your approach to problems and innovative in looking for solutions, all without worrying about what anyone else is going to think or how anyone else will be affected (since it all occurs within your own dreamworld).

Working On Creativity

Lucid dreaming may be the perfect state for artists to see what a new painting or sculpture being imagined might look like, for architects to check out new designs, or for scientists to play out experiments. It may be the perfect way for a screenwriter to see how the movie will look or a musician to listen to a new piece. In essence, lucid dreaming may be the best place for people to be creative without having to extend themselves in reality. You can purposefully play out ideas with extremely vivid imagery and few boundaries. Perhaps this is why so many writers have been able to gain ideas from their dreams, since the dream state, lucid or not, allows much greater freedom in creativity than the waking state.

Facing the Dark Side

Facing up to your fears and nightmares or conflict is another application of lucid dreaming. There are different schools of thought where this is concerned. Some who work with lucid dreams support the idea of manipulating the reality of the dreamworld in which conflict occurs and changing the dream so the nightmare images either go away or are purposefully overcome.

Facing and overcoming the monster in a dream may work in some cases, and not in others. However, as we discussed with nightmares, asking the menacing thing "What are you here for?" or "Who or what are you?" usually brings about a response and often a transformation of the image into something friendly. Remember that the images come from within yourself and therefore are representative of you. Taking advantage of lucidity in this situation will allow you to more or less be your own therapist, to identify and even work through problem areas in your life. Just remember that while this may be good for you, you may still need to deal with deep-set issues with a real therapist.

Hiding conflict or escaping from it is often a way we deny our own aggressive tendencies. According to Gayle Delaney in *Living Your Dreams* (page 172): "To confront and understand threatening or perplexing dream images is, in my opinion, the best way to approach dream guidance, because the rewards of loving and understanding your enemies seem far greater than those of demolishing them."

Reduction of anxiety by working through situations that cause such worries is very workable in lucid dreams. As the director of your own dream, you can push things in appropriate directions to show yourself that some anxieties are unfounded, while situations that cause others can be lived with or essentially fixed in waking life.

Phobias can be dealt with in lucid dreams. As controller of the dreamworld, you might bring in the thing you are afraid of and set up situations where you become more used to it, finally becoming somewhat comfortable. If you're claustrophobic, you might place your dream self in a setting that is just closed in enough to feel anxious. However, realizing you are in complete control of the reality you're in, you can begin to work with smaller and smaller enclosed spaces until your comfort level with enclosures is enough that you can face the real world with new confidence that such a setting will not adversely affect you. You are effectively healing a phobia by becoming immune to the situation that causes the fear.

Healing in Dreams

Healing the body may be an application of lucid dream imagery. Studies involving waking visualization techniques, such as Carl Simonton's work with cancer patients, indicate that positive imagery can help some people overcome illness or somehow instigate a speedier healing process within the body. Carrying that further to the lucid dream state, where just about anything is possible, the imagery and effect may be stronger than waking visualization techniques. You may be able to use the signals the body is giving you through your unconscious to recognize an illness and start the healing process; that our minds have an effect on the health of our bodies has been established. Just how the mind can work its wonders to heal us (or make us ill, for that matter) is still not understood. However, lucid dreaming may provide a more direct access to the internal workings of the mind-body connection and therefore a valuable tool in healing ourselves.

Playing in Lucid Dreams

From the more selfish end of things, lucid dreaming can be applied to simple, conscious wish fulfillment. Want to have a date (or more) with that famous movie star? Want to play at being James Bond? Want to captain the starship *Enterprise* and "boldly go where no one has gone before?" Lucid dreaming... yeah, that's the ticket. It may be the ultimate form of entertainment, as it is bound only by our imagination and is (or at least seems) participatory.

Training Yourself to Be Lucid

Of course, we do not have to control our lucid dreams to get something out of them. Merely being a conscious observer in a dream will often allow us to learn more about ourselves and ask ourselves important questions. Being an outside observer in a dream is like consciously watching a play, albeit one about our inner workings, and being able to analyze it as it goes along. We can learn much, even without direct participation (and probably can even rewind and see the instant replay if we miss something the first time).

So can we train ourselves to have a lucid dream? If so, how?

LaBerge has mentioned that even asking yourself while awake "How do I know I'm not dreaming now?" on a regular basis can program you to ask the same question while in a dream.

That suspicion, that recognition that it *may* be a dream is often enough to make you lucid in your dreams. Reminding yourself that you will both remember your dreams and be awake in them helps as well. Repeating such reminders at bedtime will often have a great impact.

There are a few methods that researchers have relayed that seem to help induce lucid dreams. The asking of the question above is a starting point. Rehearsal of a dream you'd like to have, or incubating—pondering a question with the intent of waking up in a dream to deal with it—can help program your dream state to allow for lucidity. Most crucial, however, seems to be the *intention* to be *awake* in your dreams, *recognition* of what is real and what is a dream even while awake, and *intention* of dream recall to reinforce the patterns of lucid dreaming. Using remembered dreams, going over them in your mind with the added image of you being awake or lucid in those dreams, can help set you toward that actually happening with subsequent dreams.

Keith Harary and Pamela Weintraub developed a practical program to work toward lucid dreaming. Published as *Lucid Dreams in 30 Days: The Creative Sleep Program*, the program is a step-by-step guide to train yourself to wake up in your dreams at a slow pace so as not to force the issue, and it covers dream recall as part of that process. According to Harary, the idea of a thirty-day program allows for gradual development of the ability to have lucid dreams on a regular basis and allows you to get adjusted to the process of dreaming in a conscious fashion.

Psychic in Lucid Dreams?

Lucid dreaming may allow for a conscious recognition of the extra information that may come into our minds that we've deemed psychic. If you are aware you are dreaming, you may be able to isolate psychic information or even initiate the retrieval of such information. ESP in lucid dreams is an interesting prospect, and one not really researched as yet.

If you do learn lucid dreaming, you might even use that conscious awareness to attempt telepathic contact with the dreams or conscious mind of another. Once in a lucid dream, you might suggest or state to yourself that you are powerfully psychic and proceed to seek out information on specific problems or questions using this newfound lucid dreaming psi. In the dream, act as though you have telepathy and try to contact a friend or a relative, use clairvoyance/remote viewing to peek in on an event at another location, watch a movie you've never seen, or visit a location you've never been to. Then, once awake, check the results of the dream experience with the physical reality. If the physical reality matches the dreamed information, congratulate yourself. You may have just learned how to become instantly psychic, if only in that lucid dream state. And that ability, even dreamed up, may put you one step closer toward conscious psychic experience.

You could even try to be a medium and connect with a deceased loved one.

Lucid Dreams and OBEs

One particular form of experience connected to psi that often comes up in a discussion of lucid dreaming is the out-of-body experience (OBE). LaBerge and a few others see the OBE as a very vivid form of lucid dreaming, one in which the self-image is placed outside the body and in the real world, yet where all is still a dream. The idea that the OBE may be simply a clairvoyant experience where we merely *think* we're not in our bodies may have support in the lucid dream where psi-derived information is brought in to the dreamworld. On the other hand, the view of people who have conscious OBEs like Keith Harary and the late Alex Tanous (which I and many others looking at OBEs share) is that the lucid dream and the OBE are two different states. You can have an OBE while in a lucid dream, but having such experience does not mean you are dreaming, lucid or not.

In a paper presented at the 1989 Parapsychological Association, Rex Stanford discussed a study that indicated a correlation between lucid dreaming and OBEs that take place in the dream state. There was no correlation of lucid dreaming to OBEs, as they occur in the hypnagogic or waking state. It was proposed, however, that lucidity may be some kind of launching point or bridge for the OBE, allowing the "whatever it is that leaves the body" to leave.

It is also possible that the lucid dream state gives us access to some of our own psychokinetic ability other than that of healing. There are no studies to my knowledge on this, and I really haven't heard of any such experiences, but who knows. If *you* go lucid, I'd suggest you try.

High Lucid Dreams

There are also those lucid dreams that may even transcend our awareness of the material world. Called *high lucid* dreams, these provide glimpses of what the human consciousness might evolve to through spiritual transformation, through a sense of true freedom, a oneness with the universe, and/or a knowing or a "cosmic awareness" (to quote more than a few Marvel Comics).

So What Good Are They?

Lucid dreams should not be taken lightly. As mentioned by Gackenbach and Bosveld, in and of itself, lucid dreaming is more or less a hollow accomplishment. If you don't use it for anything, what good is it? Since it may provide incredible insight into ourselves, use it for work within yourself.

In the lucid dream, we are aware of being in a dream. This may be the only definite we can get out of any state of our existence. Can we really say we are truly awake while our bodies are not asleep? At least in the lucid dream, we can say we are truly dreaming and mean it. Or is there more to the lucid dream, and to dreams in general? Are we leaving behind the body and entering a dream realm or even reentering, in some astral or spirit form, the real world?

Let's go out of body and see, shall we?

chapter 6
Dreaming Your Way Out of Your Body

Have you ever had a dream that you floated out of your body? Maybe one in which you flew to another place, either a place where you perceived friends or relatives, or a place you'd never been before? Ever think that maybe somehow the dream was true, that you really went there somehow?

How about this: Ever have the sensation while awake that you were somehow out of your body? Maybe you even felt, while awake, that you were somehow floating above your own body.

Both scenarios, the experience occurring while dreaming and the experience while awake, might be considered out-of-body experiences. As mentioned earlier, the OBE is not strictly a psychic experience, but rather a psychological one—simply the *experience* that you somehow felt yourself outside your own body. It's when you can somehow remember what you just observed while in the out-of-body state, and that information, which is not already in your memory and not available to you through your normal senses or logical inference, checks out as true. This can also be said in instances where you are out of body and are somehow seen by other living people in that state.

What Leaves the Body?

Whether something actually leaves the body is a question left up in the air at this time. In discussing the classic astral projection and astral body, some kind of spirit form leaves the corporeal body behind and can travel elsewhere, without the constraints. The astral body is often described by writers on astral projection as being tethered to the physical form by a silver cord, to prevent the astral spirit from being lost or cut off. If the cord breaks, according to these occult experts on astral projection, the astral body may not find its way back to the physical body, and the body may die or become inhabited (possessed) by another spirit.

But the majority of OBEs reported in many surveys—and I include psychics who claim controlled OBEs—don't fit the occultist mode of the astral double, so we really can't just accept the soul-leaves-body concept at face value. In fact, the majority of people who have an OBE do not report a silver cord or any cord at all, and some have even noted their surprise at *not* seeing a cord during an OBE. So what's really going on here?

As mentioned, there are also parallels between a clairvoyant or a remote-viewing experience and the OBE. The only difference appears to be that in the clairvoyant/remote viewing of a distant location, we don't visit the scene, the view comes to us. In the OBE, the same information may be attainable, but somehow part of us goes there to do the viewing. There may be little or no difference in these psychic experiences except in how the viewer perceives the way the information is gathered.

Let's say we have a person who is capable of remote viewing a distant locale like the island of Mooréa in French Polynesia (off the island of Tahiti). Let's say that person has a problem in accepting what's happening when he gets the visual impression of

Mooréa. Maybe he has a hard time accepting that the information just comes to him. But maybe he wouldn't have such a hard time accepting the information if he could seem to be there to somehow directly observe the scenery. So, his mind more or less clothes the information in an OBE; it adds the sensation that he left his body behind, visited Mooréa, and brought back the information in the form of in-person observations (and while he was there, I'm sure he had a marvelous time).

Is the psychic OBE an instance where something actually leaves the body, or is it the clairvoyant experience of someone who has a hard time taking in psychically derived observations without the act of "being there?" We don't really know for sure, but with some situations where people being visited by that OBE presence see or sense the traveler certainly suggest something is projected from the physical body.

Connecting to Telepathy

In some dream-related OBEs, people have reported seeing others who apparently have invaded their dreams, with those visiting later reporting seeing the dreamer (the one reporting the incident) while they themselves were dreaming. This may be an instance of a shared dream, a telepathic experience where the dreamers tap into the same dreamworld. In the film *Inception,* Leonardo DiCaprio was capable of entering and interacting with the dream of another. Whether you classify this as an OBE or a telepathic experience is mostly a matter of semantics.

In the famed *Nightmare on Elm Street* series, Freddie Kruger is without a body altogether (he died in a fire), which makes his existence a ghostly one, a permanent OBE. He is able to jump into and influence the dreams of others, which in turn influences their physical bodies. Again, there is a case to be made for telepathy, since it is the mind/spirit or consciousness of Freddie that enters the dream through a mental connection with the dreamer.

Something Leaves the Body?

There have been experiments in the field of parapsychology looking at the main question of whether it's ESP or OBE. In one experimental series conducted by Robert Morris, the subject of the experiment, Keith Harary, was to visit his kittens (who were in another room) while out of his body. The behavior of one of the kittens during these visits correlated with its behavior when Keith was physically present. Did the kitten actually sense Keith's presence while in the OB state, or was the kitten somehow aware Keith was thinking of being there and responding accordingly? Again, we can't say for sure (although it would seem from this and other experiments that there *was* something leaving the body). Harary, by the way, has not only written about lucid dreams, but also OBEs (*Have an Out-of-Body Experience in 30 Days*).

The American Society for Psychical Research (ASPR) conducted a series of experiments looking at OBEs for many years. The late Alex Tanous, a psychic who'd had OBEs since he was a child, was involved in those experiments from 1968 through the 1980s. The ASPR experiments, conducted by Dr. Karlis Osis and Donna McCormick, used both targets for Alex to perceive as well as physical measurements that Alex tried to affect while in the OB state, with some degree of success. [Note: If you're interested, watch a video of the experiments at the ASPR up on YouTube by searching "ASPR OBE Experiment."]

Alex's own definition of the OBE included the idea that some part of his consciousness (but not his soul or spirit) left his body.

During an interview conducted by Marvin Scott of Independent Network News (through WPIX TV in New York) in 1982 at the ASPR, Alex defined the OBE as a "separation of my consciousness from my body which is able to perceive on its own." In other words, some part of Alex's consciousness or mind would split off and "go anywhere in the world and perceive what is there and bring back the information" to his physical body. Many psychics supposedly capable of an active OBE agree with Alex on that point, and have said that only part of themselves, part of their consciousness or spirit, splits off, sort of like a space probe or psychic double. It is that double that goes elsewhere, makes observations, and returns with those memories.

When OBEs Occur

Surveys of OBEs reveal interesting statistics. Less than 5 percent of people having had an OBE have observed that silver cord connection back to their bodies. It was found that 44 percent of the experiences take place during sleep, though probably not in a deep sleep, as in a dream state. Experients having the OBE while asleep don't usually confuse the experience with a dream; they report that they feel different than normal dreams. Some OBEs in dreams may be, as Stephen LaBerge suggests, a form of a lucid dream. However, others with sleeping/OBE experiences say that while they have the OBE during a dream, and the OBE feels different than a normal dream, they are not necessarily conscious of being in a dream state or even asleep, as the definition of a lucid dream necessitates. What often tells such people that they (their bodies, at least) are asleep is that as they leave their bodies; they look down upon themselves and see themselves sleeping peacefully.

About 32 percent of the OBEs reported took place while the experients were awake but relaxed. Parapsychologist Dr. John Palmer has reported that about 28 percent take place in the hypnagogic state. A number of OBEs take place while the experient is under extreme stress, such as in surgery, in a physical accident, during illness, during a near-death experience, or even while under severe emotional duress.

The most typical OBE, whether occurring asleep-and-dreaming or awake-but-relaxed or in the almost-asleep state, is described as a floating sensation, a sensation that one is floating up near the ceiling, and often the sight of one's own body from a point floating in the air or standing by the bed. Such descriptions often come out of dreams, where the dreamer may not even classify that experience as an OBE.

Going back to Alex Tanous's definition, whatever it is that leaves the body (let's call it the "OB Something") is capable of going elsewhere in the world, without the physical body, and is capable of perceiving surroundings and events, bringing that information back to the body. That the OBE can occur while awake or asleep-and-dreaming does not diminish its capabilities in observing events and bringing information back. However, whether one can recall the OBE and the information brought back by the OB Something may clearly depend on whether one is in a dream state or not while having the OBE. If it occurs while awake or even in the hypnagogic state, there may be a greater likelihood that you will remember what you perceived while you were out. If the OBE occurs during dreaming, you may not recall much or any of the information, or it may be remembered along with (and confused with) other dream imagery, and therefore not recognized for what it was. Working on good dream recall will help with this process of determining whether you had an OBE (or other psychic experience) and with recognizing the information from the outside.

Out of Body, but Being Seen

There have been reports of OBEs during which an individual having an OBE is actually seen at a location other than where his or her physical body resides; a case of *bilocation*. These are very interesting experiences. When corroborated by witnesses at both locations, they indicate that something quite unusual and anomalous is going on. Tanous, who had been the subject of more than a decade of OBE research by the ASPR had reported such experiences which eyewitness testimony corroborated.

I've had my own experience with this as well, which ties in to dreams and OBEs. Back when I was working at the ASPR in 1982, I was also teaching parapsychology adult education courses. I became good friends with one of my students, who claimed to have real psychic ability and did healing work, and her daughter. One morning I woke up having had a very vivid dream of being at their house, which was about forty miles away. In the dream, it was late at night and I was talking with her and her daughter. A couple of days later, this same friend/student asked me if I had a dream about visiting her house on the night in question (the night I actually had the dream).

When I replied yes with a bit of puzzlement, she said that I had actually shown up there in the house after midnight while she was having a conversation with her daughter. I was seen and even somehow touched by them (and their dog reacted to me as well) at the time I was also home asleep (unless I had started sleep-driving). They were aware I was home asleep (I apparently told them), and they asked me to leave. I promptly vanished, she said.

This OBE/bilocation experience was followed two weeks later by a second one with the same friend, though in that case I was in a waking (though bored) state when I experienced the OBE, and because of a little forethought, we both took notes on the conversation specifics. When I called her, the first thing she asked was "Did you take notes, too?" Our accounts matched. Apparently, I was seemingly in two places at once.

Such bilocation OBEs do not prove that something actually leaves the body. It is also possible that the other me was a telepathic projection, a psychic image projected directly into the minds of the perceivers that had visual, auditory, and even tactile (touch) components so that it seemed as though I was physically there.

That the first time it happened to me was when I was dreaming was very interesting. Many people have seen apparitions (apparent ghosts) of people who were really still alive. In some of those living apparitional sightings, it has been reported that the subject of the apparition was asleep at the time they were seen. Some people have related such stories to me, and included that they remembered dreaming about visiting that friend or relative (who saw them).

These could be situations where someone awake telepathically picks up on the dreams of someone asleep, rather than the other way around. I'll discuss this a bit more in the chapter on telepathic dreams.

In general, most OBEs that occur while someone is dreaming are not bilocation or apparitional experiences. There is rarely someone at the other end who sees the OB traveler. These are exceptions rather than the rule.

Connecting OBEs and Dreams

The general experiences connecting dreams and OBEs include more observation on the part of the dreamer, information coming in from that distant location arrived at through an OBE. These locations are not always true representations of the actual place. People have reported many odd extras when describing Paris or New York or wherever else they had traveled to in the dream OBE. Somehow the places are modified.

The places people travel to while in the OBE are not always true physical locations. People have reported strange worlds or settings, which often sound similar to the kind of imagery one would have in a dream. Some people find themselves in worlds similar to but slightly different from their normal physical surroundings, or sometimes somehow capable of making changes to their surroundings, of manipulating whatever reality they seem to have entered in the OB state.

Have they truly entered other realities, an astral plane, or maybe traveled through time itself? Have they entered parallel worlds just slightly different than our own? Or are these perceptions of different realities merely reflections of a dream state? Such imagery does make it difficult to decide where the OBE leaves off and the dream takes precedence, if there is an OBE at all.

So, in essence, while it may be very difficult to tease the OBE away from the dream as a separate experience (when the OBE occurs during sleep), it may not really matter. In the end, it would be wonderful if we could really understand that the OBE is or isn't a situation in which something actually leaves the body. At the present, however, we are stuck with really not knowing this.

Add to that dilemma the OBE as it occurs within a dream, and you place that experience in a setting that further confounds the question. No longer is it simply a matter of "Is the OBE a clairvoyant experience dressed up as a venture outside the physical body or is it a case of the astral body or spirit or consciousness actually separating from the physical body?" When the OBE occurs within the dream state, we add to that question the imagery of the unconscious, which can dress up psychic information and deep memory as a psychic experience or an excursion to another place or time.

The ultimate question for our time, since we really have no objective means to discover whether something truly leaves the body or not, is "Does it matter?"

In all cases, whether the information is coming from "traveling clairvoyance" or the OBE or a psychic dream dressed up as a voyage to another location, it is presented in a way that is saying to us "Hey, take a look at this. It may be important to you!"

So, what you might do when you have such dreams, which may or may not be OBEs, is to simply consider the information presented and its usefulness to you. It may be that the information seems frivolous and not very useful—maybe it was fun info, your mind just throwing you something to make you smile—or it may have been frightening and indicative of some other deep problem or question in your life.

In any case, the information bears paying attention to, regardless of how it bubbled up through the layers of your consciousness, or whether you had to go out of your body to get it. If the OBE is some form of clairvoyance, a disguise for another form of psychic experience, do we experience clairvoyance differently? Or do we have the out-of-body sensation when we gain information from other locations?

The answer is in the absence of that sensation, as you'll see very soon.

chapter 7
Dreams of Days Past:
Reincarnation

Have you ever had a dream of being in some past time, some historical setting that took place before the year of your birth? Ever wonder where it came from or whether somehow you could really have been there?

There has been much discussion for years about past lives and reincarnation. More than a billion people on the planet believe, and even US television started taking a look at cases of children recalling past lives in the reality series *Ghost Inside My Child* (an ill-fitting title, but a decent show). Many believe that our wisdom or lack thereof, our likes and dislikes, and even our problems are related to our past lives, and past life regression therapy has become a successful tool in the hypnotherapists kit. Psychics and channelers are asked routinely to describe the past lives of their clients. And our dreams, we are told, often let information about such past lives slip into our consciousness.

Reincarnation Belief

Reincarnation, the idea that our soul, spirit, or consciousness can be reborn in a new body and given a fresh start, is not new. In fact, the idea is right up there with any other idea of an afterlife, and whole religions (such as Hinduism) make it a central belief, often including the idea that one can come back not only as a human, but as any living creature under the sun (or under the ground or sea, for that matter).

The belief was even part of early Christian teachings. According to some scholars of the many versions of the Bible, the belief in reincarnation was excised from the teachings of Christ and the Apostles in the fourth century AD by the second Catholic Congress convened by the Emperor Theodosius; a political decision, not necessarily a religious one. Apparently, belief in a second chance after one dies makes it difficult to control people (from a political standpoint). In other words, "if you sin in this life, you still get another chance" is not a concept that helps keep people as well-behaved as "if you sin in this life you will suffer eternal damnation."

So, the idea has been around (and reborn into more than a few cultures and religions from time to time). The question of *evidence* and *proof* arises when one studies the concept.

The Problem of Proof

There are a few proof sources cited by people who believe in reincarnation. One is the idea that the religions that teach its existence are correct, and that it does happen, thanks to God or the gods or whomever else one's religion says may be in charge of the universe. "So it is written" is a familiar argument for a lot of religious ideas. Arguing against such belief system proof sources is just about impossible, scientifically or otherwise, unless one can prove or disprove the idea of a particular god or gods or God.

A more common proof source brought up since the 1950s is the idea of past life regression, or using hypnosis or other techniques to regress a person's memories to a time before conception. Many people have remembered some kind of existence in the fairly recent or extremely distant past. Most of these past identities are either unverifiable or too verifiable. How do you verify if there was a wise-man from Atlantis named Arion if we can't even verify the existence of Atlantis as a real, though sunken, place? How can there be several people running around all claiming to be the same famous person in a past life?

The big problem with hypnotic regression is information contamination. There is no way to absolutely exclude all a person has read, seen, heard, or experienced as far as information about the past is concerned. Someone who swears never to have read or heard anything about County Cork in Ireland in the late nineteenth century, yet remembers a fairly convincing past life (complete with accent) may have come into contact with such information without remembering the information source.

We all gather relatively useless or innocuous information from the world around us on a daily basis. Conversations from others do enter our ears and lodge in long-term (though undoubtedly submerged) memory, whether we are conscious of hearing that information or not. Who among us can truly and honestly say that we can remember *everything* we ever read or saw on TV or in a movie, especially while we were children? Can we truly remember that Irish neighbor of ours from the time we were three years old, the one who used to babysit and tell us bedtime stories of her life in County Cork?

Information lodged in our subconscious memory is still retrievable information, especially while in an altered state of consciousness, such as in a hypnotic trance. For whatever reason—often the suggestion of the hypnotherapist that we really did have a past life—our minds come up with that information, creating a past life that sounds interesting to us (and certainly to the hypnotherapist).

Past life regression is not valid proof of reincarnation. In fact, because of the problem of information contamination, it stinks from a parapsychological viewpoint. It's interesting, but not very useful. There are uses for it, however.

The Pluses of Past Life Metaphors

As a therapeutic tool, past life regression may be very valuable. For some people, getting at what bugs us is a problem. If we can set the cause of problems in the context of "it was an issue in a past life that is causing problems today," we can remove ourselves from any responsibility for that problem and allow the unconscious to present the issues in a metaphorical way. "I have relationship problems today because of what happened to me in my last lifetime." Such discussion of the past life and problems can reveal much to a therapist, in the way any sort of association or storytelling therapy might work, such as Jungian sand tray therapy, or as in dreamwork.

Regression therapy can be a powerful tool as far as brief therapy techniques are concerned. Often we are unable to address our inner problems or even recognize them, and such regression to a past life—real or imagined—can allow for both a way to perceive the issues somewhat distanced from ourselves as we are now and to come up with creative ways to deal with those issues.

Past Life Readings

People visiting psychics and channelers are often told about their past lives. Assuming the psychic or channeler is truly psychic and even capable of piercing the veil of time to the past, what they are picking up may or may not be real information. Maybe they are capable of focusing on some part of you that reveals who you were in the past, and maybe not. Again, verification is extremely difficult if you are told you were an Egyptian slave or a dolphin in that past life. Or perhaps what the psychic/channeler is doing is picking up on problems or concerns of your life today, revealing that information to you in the form of a metaphor, a story with something to say about what you need to do with your life right *now*.

So if there is no real evidential information, nothing verifiable, is the psychic coming up with something that is more than pure entertainment? My advice is to discard the window dressing of the story of the past life and look closely at the actual advice being given. If it doesn't sound right, think twice about it (and please use good old common sense, as well as your own intuition).

Reincarnation and Parapsychology

There actually are well-researched and investigated cases of re-incarnation, though ultimately they're only strongly suggestive or extremely supportive, not absolute proof. To avoid the kind of lifetime information contamination mentioned above, young children, with little exposure to the information that would allow them to create the past life, are often the best sources of such cases. There are literally thousands of cases of children under the age of five that suddenly and spontaneously remember having lived before as someone else. The vast majority of reported cases come from countries such as India, Burma, Sri Lanka, Thailand, and others where reincarnation is part of the actual belief system, though more and more quite excellent cases have been coming from Western sources. The preponderance of past cases from India and Southeast Asia is more than likely because in cultures and religions that don't recognize reincarnation, or see it as too weird, the parents of a three-year-old speaking about a past life would most likely first assume that the child's imagination is at work rather than literally believe what the child is saying could be factual.

Dr. Ian Stevenson of the University of Virginia was the preeminent researcher/writer in this area from the 1950s until his death in 2007, with his banner taken up at UVA by Dr. Jim Tucker. There are cases with the children providing rich detail of that past life that have been investigated by researchers under Stevenson's auspices and subsequent to his death. Checking the information for accuracy, then checking for possible information contamination is part of this investigative process.

Children (the younger the better) are good sources for such cases, not just because the chances of contamination are much less, but also the memories may be stronger simply because the child hasn't grown up enough to establish a personality or self-identity. In some cases, the children have been able to speak in the dialect or language of the person whom they supposedly were in that past life.

The information coming from such children is far and away much more suggestive of reincarnation than either hypnotic regression or information from psychics. Adding in the dialect/

language matches makes it even better. A person capable of remembering a past life (in hypnosis or spontaneously) who is also capable of speaking and *conversing* in the language or dialect of both the geographic location and the time period adds much to overcome the information contamination possibility.

Adults often report such spontaneous recollections, but due to the increased chance of contamination, as well as the slight possibility of some form of multiple personality disorder that feeds off information from the subconscious or a psychic possibility, such cases are relatively low on the proof (or even evidence) totem pole. However, that psychic possibility, retrocognition (reaching into the past for information of which you are not aware), may be responsible for a number of these cases, including many of the cases involving children.

Retrocognition

Retrocognition is a natural outgrowth of the idea of precognition, awareness of the future. After all, even though there are many concepts of how time works with regards to the future, we know (or at least we think we know) that there is a past to gain information from.

Cases of reincarnation may be cases of retrocognition, of reaching back for detailed information. Once the information is received, the mind may clothe that information in a neat package of memory, in much the same way information gained by clairvoyance is turned into an out-of-body experience. Your mind has a hard time accepting the observations of that past event unless you were somehow there, so it creates the context of a past life to provide a vehicle for passing the information on to you.

It is unlikely, though possible, that personality quirks and mannerisms would come to someone via retrocognition. It is more unlikely that language could be received to such a degree as to make the person conversant. While such language-rich cases are rare in the reincarnation literature, they're not unheard of. These cases, above all the others, are more strongly supportive of reincarnation, and less so of retrocognition.

Real-Time ESP and Imprints

If there are records or information in existence that allow us to check the memories of a past life against historical fact, it is also possible that ostensible cases of reincarnation and even retrocognition are real-time clairvoyance of those records, not memories of a past life or retrocognition of past events.

Such information comes out in a variety of ways. For example, let's say that you had an acquaintance living in a very old house (Revolutionary War period) in the northeast United States. You visit that person for dinner, discussing a number of things, but little or nothing about the house and its history. That night, you have a dream, which you remember the next morning. In the dream, you observed several people looting the house after taking away the inhabitants at gunpoint. They were all dressed in clothing of the eighteenth century. In the dream, you saw the man taken from the house try to run, to escape, and you watched as he was shot down.

Sometime in the next few days, you speak with the acquaintance who lives in the house, and relate the dream to him, starting out with a typical "I had a wonderful time, and I even had a weird dream about the house." The person you're relating this to is puzzled. He didn't tell you about the house's history or that the original owner's family were Tories and arrested by the Continental Army, or that the owner tried to escape and was shot. You and all others at that dinner also agree that there was no such discussion. So how did you know? And why do you suddenly feel like you've fallen into *The Twilight Zone* (cue the music).

Most people are aware of psychics who can read the history of an object by holding it in their hands. This is an offshoot of clairvoyance that is sometimes called psychometry. The concept is that objects can record information—that happenings around an object are imprinted on it—and can be deciphered by our brains. The information can be effectively played back in a variety of ways, and may be far from complete. But in many reported experiences, the playback may be like that of a DVR, with the psychic watching the events from the past as though watching a film or video. Of course, it's not just self-professed psychics who have these experiences. Most of us have such experiences many times in our lives.

Ever go into a house for the first time and feel like you were very much at home there, that it felt like a good place? Or the reverse, you felt very uncomfortable, like something bad had happened there (which may have simply been the folks living there having very emotional fights)? Picking up on the vibes of a house or other location or even such perceptions of antiques or other previously owned items seems to point to our capability to receive information apparently imprinted on that object.

There is little difference between perceiving the history of a handheld object or a house you walk into. What is a house but a large object?

All this might take place during waking consciousness, or be perceived and taken in through our subconscious, only to come out during sleep and dreaming.

Imprints in Dreams

So the subconscious mind, which has this great information to relay to us, chooses another avenue that the conscious mind can deal with: dreams. Placing the information in a dream allows for either acceptance of the information as is, as having been picked up from the house or object. It more often allows you to dismiss the information as just a dream, which is much less threatening.

In any event, whether a single dream is a case of retrocognition, of viewing the past, or of some clairvoyant, real-time reading of the information picked up by an object or location is impossible to determine at the present time. Again, it doesn't matter what label we place on it. If the information is useful or interesting, make use of it, enjoy the experience. Whether there is a direct link with the past or whether you're decoding existing information really only matters to the people studying the experiences. If all retrocognition is psychometry or clairvoyance of records, it may mean we cannot psychically pick up information through time (at least to the past). That helps researchers and theorists in looking for and understanding psi processes, but probably doesn't mean a whole lot as far as the person having the experience is concerned.

From a spiritual perspective, whether we're remembering an actual past life through our dreams or conscious experience, or whether we're having psychic access to information in the past or recorded in the past, it does matter to what's happening here. Unfortunately, you've seen that there are too many unanswered questions and alternate interpretations to have an answer to what's happening here.

Dreaming Past Life Memories

In their dreams, people do have remembrances or experiences of being someone else. So, too, do they occasionally bring forth verifiable information about past events and people. In fact, dreams can work well as a vehicle for our memories to remind us of something important we may not be able to dredge up consciously. Similar to other psychic dreams, sometimes there is verifiable information, that which can be researched and confirmed (or denied). The subjective experience of the dreamer that the dream actually represented a past life must be considered and added to support that this is a reincarnation-related experience.

Unfortunately, as with spontaneous waking experience of a potential past life, a lifetime of information contamination for adults lessens the value of the experience as real evidence for the past life (or for clairvoyance or retrocognition). But it does not lessen the experience for the dreamer.

The important lesson to be learned is that these memories, these experiences, and these dreams may have much to tell us about ourselves and how we need to view ourselves and our connections with other people in our lives today. It's the information's validity and applicability that we need to concern ourselves with, not whether we lived before in Atlantis. After all, as far as Atlantis is concerned, you really can't go home again … except in your dreams.

The past is what we call the present after it has happened. The present is when we live now. Psychic experiences of the present are therefore easier to look at, since we're there now.

chapter 8
Sharing Your Dreams: Telepathy

Telepathy is one of those abilities used and abused by the movies and television, in science fiction and comic books, as well as by speculators of military applications of psi. The idea that one person can gain an awareness of what's in another's mind is at the same time both more and less than what most people think of when they hear the word *telepathy*. It's not mind reading and it's not a direct communications link-up of two minds—though there can be mutual or shared experiences, especially in dreaming. No one can directly and deeply access the mind, the thoughts, the emotions of another, at least as far as we know. If such a person were to exist, it's unlikely that he or she would step forward to disclose that ability. It would probably freak most of us out.

Experiences of telepathy seem to revolve around a basic awareness of the general contents of another's thoughts or emotions. One person is having a particular train of thought or maybe is in a particular emotional state, and the other person has a sudden "knowing" of this and gets the gist of what the sender is thinking or feeling. The exception to this concept is demonstrated in a medium's communications with a spirit, as this is purely mental interaction. Even if the medium says she is hearing a voice of a spirit, it's still happening in the mind; it's telepathic.

People are interested in such connections between people, especially people related to one another (such as mother and child or twins) or very close emotionally (husband and wife or lovers). There are a couple of considerations when looking at the apparent telepathic experiences of people who are so close.

Connections

First of all, one must always consider the non-psychic connection. People who have lived together for a long time (not just in a relationship ... this also fits the twins and the parent/child connections) or who simply have really gotten to know each other well in certain situations can often predict how each other will respond in similar situations. I frequently hear "We often know what each other is thinking" ... "Sometimes I can start a sentence and s/he can finish it." One must always consider that two people who know each other well, who have been through many kinds of situations together, might really know just how each other will respond in a particular situation, even to understanding basically what the other would say in that situation. This is not usually a conscious thing.

The other point to take into consideration is that emotion seems to play a big part in psychic experience in general. Two (or more) people emotionally involved often seem to share some sort of above-average psychic linkup. It's not just that twins are more psychic because of the genetics involved, but rather because of an emotional tie between them.

Telepathic information rears its head in many situations. For example, there are many stories of people knowing when someone close to them is in a crisis, in danger, or even when such a person has died. It may be that the person in crisis sends out a telepathic cry of alarm. Those who get it clearest (if at all) are generally the same people who are normally empathetic about friends, lovers, and relatives.

In Dreams

Telepathic information sharing also seems to occur when in the dream state. Not only do people sometimes dream of others they know in particular situations, later to find that those situations were actually going on at the time of the dream (or were thought about by the person dreamed about), but there are reports of shared dreams—of two people having the same dream.

There has been much work in the field of parapsychology on telepathic dreams. The seminal work is *Dream Telepathy* by Montague Ullman and Stanley Krippner with Alan Vaughan. The work was conducted at Maimonides Medical Center in New York during the sixties, although analyses of telepathic dreaming continue today, and are reported in parapsychological journals from time to time (*Journal of Parapsychology, Journal of Scientific Exploration, Journal of the Society for Psychical Research,* and in the past in the *Journal of the American Society for Psychical Research*). The work at Maimonides stands as an exceptionally rich body of experimental data that supports a psi hypothesis.

Experiments conducted in dream telepathy have typically included protocols similar to other psi experiments, though with the addition of the sleep/dream factor. Participants designated as receivers were asleep at the time the senders were focusing on the targets. By monitoring the sleep stages of receivers, researchers were able to watch for dreaming (REM sleep), then wake up the receivers as they exited that stage. Since people can remember their dreams best when awakened just after REM, the subjects were able to describe their dreams for the researchers, often in great detail. In the Maimonides experiments, the verbal descriptions were recorded and later transcribed. The description of the dream would be matched up by judges with the targets. In many instances, the connections between the detailed descriptions and the targets were more than obvious.

Judging the Hits

One of the difficulties in doing any experiment where there is no forced target, such as with card guessing, is the addition of details or the attempt to identify imagery and other information by the mind of the receiver. While there may be several similarities between what the receiver describes and what the target is, the target is often placed into the context of a dream, sometimes making it difficult to tease it apart from the additional details of the dream, with the dream imagery masking the psi signal.

For example, let's say the target, Bob, is concentrating on a picture of a robin perching on the limb of a tree. The receiver, Fred, has a dream about Batman and Robin, both looking over Gotham City by standing (perching?) on the ledge of a building. Is this a hit? Well, while it may seem obvious to you that there is a connection between the picture of a robin and the dream of Batman's partner, Robin, perched on the edge of something, we might have to look at other possibilities.

Did Fred recently see any movies or TV shows with Robin featured alongside the Caped Crusader? Does Fred read comic books? Has he had other dreams about superheroes, or specifically about Batman and Robin?

Even if any of these other sources of dream information are pertinent, the timing of the dream in connection with the timing of that particular target suggestion still may yield statistical significance. Or there may be another problem. If the judges looking at target pictures end up with targets that include a robin and a picture of, say, Batman or some other superhero, the judge may have difficulty in choosing between the two potential targets. How would you choose if the dream was of Batman and Robin, and your target choices were a picture of a robin and a picture of a superhero?

You can see that unless one is careful about target selection and judging, we might have a problem in deciding on an impartial basis that any particular target had a connection with a particular dream. Fred's mind might have simply received the picture of the robin (bird) and processed it into a dream about Robin (the Boy Wonder). That doesn't mean that Fred did not *get* the correct target, just that the process of dreaming may embellish the information, placing it into totally different contexts.

Telepathy vs. Clairvoyance

On top of all this, you have the added problem of whether this is truly telepathy or really clairvoyance. Is the source of information the sender's mind or is it the target picture itself? This is, at this point in time, difficult if not impossible to answer. But, once again, does it really matter if it's telepathy or clairvoyance? There is psi happening here, and that may be the only truly important consideration. Later, when researchers in parapsychology have a handle on the process of these two abilities (if they are in fact separate abilities), this question will be of more importance, and perhaps easier to answer.

So what is a true telepathic experience? Couldn't any experience be clairvoyant? To a great degree, the answer to the second question is yes, in that if there is an event or an experience, a stimulus in physical reality that causes the sender to think or send that information, the receiver may be focusing on the stimulus rather than the mind of the sender. If the information is simply mental, if what is being broadcast is simply a thought, emotion, or memory, with no relation to the sender's environment, then we can say we're probably dealing with telepathy and telepathy alone.

Telepaths!

Deanna Troi, the counselor aboard the starship *Enterprise* on *Star Trek: The Next Generation,* is a member of a people who are true telepaths. In episodes where Troi's mother shows up, communication between mother and daughter is presented as purely mental discussion, though Troi typically insists that they verbalize (telepathy can apparently be considered rude behavior by those of us who can't do it). Troi, however, had a father from Earth, a nontelepathic human. Consequently, unlike her mother and other Betazoids, her abilities are genetically diluted. She cannot pick up stray thoughts from other nontelepathic people. She can, however, pick up emotional states, even over a great distance (such as from people in another starship). This empathic ability to pick up emotions from others makes her an excellent counselor for folks with emotional or psychological disturbances, or even just for people who have a hard time with a particular decision.

Star Trek has illustrated many such examples of telepathic ability throughout all the various series, as has science fiction in general. Even more dramatic and comedy films and TV shows have done this, especially those in which ghosts appear who can still communicate with the living (which is telepathy), even films like *Just Like Heaven,* in which Reese Witherspoon's character, out of body while her body is in a coma, communicates with Mark Ruffalo. Professor X of *The X-Men* comics and films is a true telepath. The movie *What Women Want* is a fun comedy all about mind reading. But that's all fiction, of course.

Not a Clear Channel, But Direct

Telepathy as mind-to-mind communication is far from a desired form of interaction the way we experience it today. We cannot simply think a message to others and expect it to be received (that's what texting is for). Our subconscious minds, or whatever it is in us that controls psi, apparently do use telepathy from time to time as a form of communication. In daily life, there are instances where perhaps the reason you and another person thought the same thing at the same time was because of telepathy. Or maybe you knew who was on the other end of that ringing phone because you picked up on that person's thoughts centering on you. Or maybe the reason why that long-lost buddy of yours even called you to begin with was because you were thinking of him and he picked up on that (or vice versa ... you picked up on his thoughts of you, leading you to think of him, leading to an awareness of "that's Fred calling now").

Since direct communication from mind to mind is considered telepathy, it may be that one person's dream can be recognized as possibly telepathic by another. For example, Carl Jung and other therapists since Jung, including Nandor Fodor and Jule Eisenbud, have reported clients' dreams that seemingly tap into the therapist's life. It appears that the client is telepathically picking up on some of the thoughts, emotions, and concerns of the therapist. The information is revealed to the client by including it in a dream. The fact that the only way the dream can be pegged as potentially psychic is by the therapist him/herself to whom the dream is told and not by the client who dreamed it is very interesting from a psychological point of view.

Telepathy in Dreams

You might have all sorts of interesting dreams about friends or relatives, yet not consider them anything out of the ordinary until you reveal that dream to the other person, who might respond with "Hey, that just happened to me!" or "I had the same exact dream!" Because we learn that dreams are just typically that, dreams, we often may not connect the information in a dream to a real event until after we discuss the dream with another person.

In many cases, however, you might learn of a telepathic connection without discussing a dream with another person. It may just be that the description of a situation in the life of another is enough to register that. Here are a couple of letters that illustrate this. The first comes from Joanne Mied, a psychic practitioner in northern California:

I worked with this woman, Yvette, and I dreamed one night that she had moved to Oregon. We were having dinner at her house, and there was this beautiful stream and a waterfall right outside the window. She really liked living there, she had lost weight, she didn't work, she could stay home all the time, and she was really happy.

The next morning, I came in and said, "Hey, Yvette, I had this dream about you." She said that that night her husband had come home and told her that this company had

been thinking about moving to Oregon. If they moved there,
she wouldn't have to work.

It turned out the company was not moving, so that made it a
telepathic dream, not a precognitive one. Joanne apparently
picked up on Yvette's husband's announcement about Oregon
and played it back to herself through a dream.

Here's one with a bit of a practical value:

I was supposed to meet my mother in town. I overslept and
"awoke" to a dream of my mother knocking on my window
and telling me to "come on, R—, come on."

When I awoke, I looked at my watch. The time was 10:15
a.m. As soon as I got to the meeting, my mom told me that
at about 10:15 she had gone outside and repeatedly said
"Come on, R—, come on."

—G. S., California

It's possible that the timing of the dream and when G. S.'s mother
said she'd gone outside to wait for him and effectively call to him
was purely coincidental. It is, however, interesting to note the reported wording of the message that appeared in the dream and
in real life, and that the dream was potent enough to wake G. S.
up, which meant that while G. S. was going to be late, he wasn't
going to miss the meeting altogether.

Another example:

After my ex-husband and I were separated for five months,
I dreamed that he came to see me. About a week before he
actually came, I started having the dream again. He came

three days before Christmas and left the day before Christmas. I asked him why he didn't call before he came and he just said, "You knew I would be coming anyway." I dismissed any thought of what I had been having as a premonition simply because it was the holidays and he wanted to see his son (not quite two years old yet).

May came along and the same thing happened as with Christmas. I dismissed the idea because it was his son's birthday on May 24. He came a few days before his birthday, then, again the beginning of the next month. Each time I asked him why he didn't call and his response was the same.

A year had passed with no visits and no dreams.

In June of the following year, I began having the dreams again. Father's Day was coming up and I knew he'd be here. He never wrote or called beforehand, nor had I received any previous letters except two cards and a present for my son the previous Christmas.

My son and I packed up and went to Green Bay the weekend of Father's Day. When we returned, we heard my ex in the house. He was there looking for us.

I haven't had the dreams since 1979, nor has there been a visit from my ex since. I think my psychic abilities died with any feelings I had for him, though I think I would know if he died. I hoped he would never come to visit after that last visit.

I think he knew we had a psychic connection between us, but we never discussed it.

—C. W., Wisconsin

C. W. may very well have had a psychic connection with her ex-husband. Her awareness of his visits may actually have coincided with his planning such trips, mentally, if not in fact. There may be other factors at work here, since the dreams occurred for a bit before each visit. A very telling pointer here is her lack of dreams in connection with his lack of visits. Emotional bonds appear to create psychic ties between people. Breaking or weakening those emotions may eradicate the psychic connection.

Here's one that's a bit different, taking us to a whole other area of telepathic experience and dreams:

On April 11, 1982, I dreamed I was in an area resembling a World War II army camp, with one-story, wooden barracks. As I stood outside the building, Bob, a man I had been engaged to fourteen years earlier, walked out the door accompanied by several people I did not clearly see. He paused and looked at me in a sad, wistful manner, then slowly turned and walked away.

On the night of April 12, I had the same dream, repeated in exact detail.

On the night of April 13, the dream was repeated to the point of him pausing to look at me. In this one he said, "Sorry, honey, but this time you will be the one left behind and hurt." He turned and vanished.

In October of that year, I learned that he had been ill and died in a VA hospital on April 13, 1982.

—L. V., Washington

Was this a case of an apparition visiting a dream of a living person, a *visitation dream*? Or was this a telepathic goodbye between two old friends?

In this case, as it was a repeated dream, it would appear that Bob, who lay ill in the VA hospital, connected somehow with L. V.'s dreams. The day he died, the dream's detail shifted slightly, as though it was his way of providing a final exit line. It would be advantageous to know the time of Bob's death in relation to when L. V. dreamed the message in order to place the dream either before or after Bob actually died.

Ghostly Visitors to Our Dreams: Still Telepathy

Visitation dreams, in which a deceased person seemingly visits the living in a dream (instead of while the living person is awake), are not uncommon and do effectively fall under the telepathic dreams header. As the majority of ghost sightings are actually at or just after the moment of death, it may be that the apparition is appearing in a dream because the person the deceased wishes to visit is already asleep. According to the experiences of those seeing such apparitions, most of these visitors are showing up to deliver a last message or to say goodbye to friends or relatives. Such goodbyes can often be a comfort to the living, as they may help reduce grief.

Many questions have come up over the years with regard to apparitional sightings. Although some may seem a bit silly, they are actually worth wondering about.

Some of them are: "Why do ghosts have clothes on and where do they get them from?" or "How is it I can see the ghost but not everyone can?" or "If the ghost is immaterial, how is it he/she can speak, since talking involves air forced through vocal cords?"

or "How is it the ghost can change appearance to some degree, appearing at different ages each day?" These questions all have to do with the actual essence of what an apparition is. Apparitions appear to look like the people they were in life, and in fact may be apparitions of living people, some form of an OBE.

In a case I investigated first in 1985 in Livermore, California, a young boy was communicating with a ghost named Lois, who was the previous owner of the house built in 1917. Lois had lived in that house all her life and died in it as well. Why was she in the house? According to the boy, she was there because she loved her house and didn't see the need to go anywhere else. She appeared to him as an old woman, a preteen, a teenager, and a woman in her twenties, often wearing different clothing on different days. He was a bright kid, and he had the presence of mind to ask how that was possible. Her answer fits with some theories about apparitions. She appeared to him in the way she wanted, in whatever her self-image was for that day, projecting that information directly into his mind.

In other words, how she felt on a given day (as a teenager, an old woman, etc.) affected what she mentally broadcast as her appearance. Her voice was part of this projection. Telepathically, there was a connection between the boy and Lois, one for which she was somehow responsible.

If some part of the human consciousness survives the death of the body, then the normal channels of communication have been cut off. No physical body is there to be seen or heard. Whether the apparition appears in the waking state of the observer or in a dream, the mode of communication would appear to be telepathy.

In the dream situations, what may happen is something like this: Susan goes to sleep one night. Unbeknownst to her, her grandfather has a heart attack and dies during that time period. Susan wakes up, remembering a dream in which her grandfather came to visit her. In the dream, her grandfather appeared to her, smiled, and said, "Don't you worry about me. I'm headed somewhere wonderful." He vanishes. Upon awakening and learning of her grandfather's death during the night, Susan is surprised, but feels that it really was her grandfather saying goodbye. While she grieves, she isn't overcome with grief, feeling he really is at rest somewhere "wonderful."

In some of the dreams of this type, the setting of the dream is much like reality, the bedroom or sleeping place of the dreamer. In others, as with L. V.'s above, the apparition appears in a dream with some other scene or surroundings more appropriate to a dream. However, there is usually an explicit or implied message that the person represented in the dream is dead or is going away somehow.

Is it possible that the apparitions of these people are tapping into the dreams of others? If you accept the possibility of apparitions at all, or the possibility that OBEs are representative of *something* leaving the body, then it follows that an apparition's presence can be registered by the mind in a conscious state or by the subconscious, dreaming part of the mind. The apparition projects his/her image or message into the mind of the dreamer, as he/she would into the mind of a conscious individual. The subconscious then takes over, placing the projected information into the context of a dream.

Or Is It the Dreamer Being Aware of the Death, Not a Spirit?

The other side of the coin here is that the telepathy of the dreamer registers the thoughts of the person dying. That person may have thought of a number of close friends and relatives before death and sent out a kind of telepathic farewell. The person(s) receiving the information processes it and places it into some context that can be accepted. If receiving it while awake, the recipient may see or experience the information as an apparition, or simply a feeling that something has happened to the person who has just died. If receiving it while asleep, the information may be integrated into the imagery of a dream, or may even cause a particular dream to happen.

We come back to the question of "What is the source of the information ... mind or event?" And again, there is no absolute answer. There may be no way of telling, short of the feeling that you, the dreamer, have when you recall the dream. Did it feel as though you were watching an event happen or did it feel as though there was an intention, a thought, a cry for help, or attention involved?

What to Do ...

What you do to assimilate such information into your life is the important issue. When you have such experiences, look to what they say to you, the dreamer. They may be telling you simply that the person was thinking of you, or that you were capable of picking up information from the other person's mind. Or they may be providing you with an emotional outlet, a preparation for some event already in the awareness of the person who "sent" the message. Or perhaps they provide information to be acted upon, like "Help me ... here's where I am" or "You're late ... wake up and get over here quick" or "I'm thinking of you and want you to call me."

There's no quick test to see if a particular dream is telepathic or not for many of them. The best kind of dreams that fall easily into the telepathy category are those that seem shared. You have a dream with a particular content, story and setting, and when you share it with someone, it turns out that he or she had the same or incredibly similar dream. There's no other source of the sharing other than what's in either or both of your heads.

Compare your dreams with those of others who may have a connection to what you dream about. Check with people you dream about and see if there is some correlation to what you dreamed, something that may say why you dreamed it. Pay attention to how the dream feels to you, whether it feels like a connection to others or something else.

Human beings, like other social animals, have a need for affiliation with others, which can definitely come out as a connection in our dreams. It all boils down to the idea that we are all more alike than different, that communication does flow, whether verbally or telepathically, from one mind to another and back.

chapter 9
Dreams of the Here and Now: Clairvoyance

Labels and classifications of words like *clairvoyance, retrocognition*, and *precognition* are a help as well as a hindrance. Getting too caught up in them confuses the issue and can make something very interesting too much trouble to deal with. With dreams, those labels can be even more confusing.

It's All about Timing

How do we tell if the psychic information is of the present (clairvoyance), of the past (retrocognition), or of the future (precognition)? You need to relate the time you had the experience to the actual time of the event. If the event happened before your experience, it was retrocognitive. If it happened after, precognitive. If it happened at the same time, clairvoyant.

With many experiences it may be virtually impossible to determine if the information crossed time as well as space. If the time difference between the perception of the information and the actual event was large (say hours, days, or even years), it wouldn't be difficult to classify that experience. If the time difference were, say, minutes or even seconds, unless that event actually happened where you were standing (or sitting) awake, there would be no way of determining that it was not a clairvoyant, real-time experience.

If a psi-viewed event occurs while you're sleeping, not knowing just when during that specific sleep period the dream happened means that you can't determine at all whether the dream was real-time or of the past or future. More importantly, even if you feel the dream was unusual and even perhaps psychic, it still may not be a dream you can immediately relate to an event.

It's best not to get that hung up on the labels.

Clairvoyance: The Now

Clairvoyance is very easy to test in the laboratory. One need simply have the target selected (randomly, and without anyone knowing the nature of that randomly assigned and hidden target), the subject make a guess, and the guess compared to the actual target.

When you add in another person staring at or concentrating on the target, the possibility that telepathy is involved comes up (did the information come from the person's mind or from the target?). As mentioned in the last chapter, if you try to set up a telepathy experiment with a target, sender, and receiver, you again confound the experiment: Is the receiver getting the information from the mind of the sender (telepathy) or from the target alone (clairvoyance)?

Remote Viewing

One of the most productive forms of experiments for clairvoyance (and precognition) research has been remote viewing. Experiments conducted in the past have used a couple of methodologies. In one, a person is sent out to the randomly selected location at the time the viewer is to receive impressions of that location. This outbound observer or beacon spends time walking around the location, noting details and focusing on what he or she observes. The viewer reveals what kinds of impressions are received from the location of the beacon.

In another real-time remote viewing methodology, experimenters randomly select location coordinates and simply ask the viewer to use them to zero in on the target and describe it.

In the first methodology, the remote viewing session includes information from a location with an observer. With such conditions, technically telepathy might be involved. In the second, we presuppose that not having an observer, a beacon, eliminates the telepathy possibility. This may not be the case, for if there are any people (or maybe even animals) in the vicinity of the selected location, the information received could have also come from them.

Do Labels Matter?

The real question is, does it matter? If the information comes in through a process that doesn't involve the normal senses or intuitive or logical inference or deduction, psi seems to be happening, regardless of whether we label it as telepathy or clairvoyance. Labels or jargon can be a problem in having people conceptualize just what it is to be psychic. People are often more caught up in whether that psi experience was telepathy or clairvoyance, rather than simply whether something unusual and informative, perhaps something psychic, did occur. Just looking at how people love to separate the "clairs" (clairvoyance, clairaudience, etc.) is a clear illustration of this.

This confusion between telepathy and clairvoyance has even carried over to precognition. Many experiments have been conducted in precognitive remote viewing, where the beacon is sent out to a location randomly selected *after* the viewer has made his/her descriptions. In some instances, the observer sent out is the actual viewer himself.

As far as psychic dreams are concerned, this same confusion could occur if you try to label or classify the dream so as to be strictly telepathic or clairvoyant.

For example, let's say I had a dream that a major world leader was being attacked. I wake up, remembering the dream, and listen to the news. I learn that an attack, such as the one I dreamed, actually took place during the night. Did I pick up that information from the actual event (clairvoyance) or from the mind of the attacker (telepathy) or even from the mind(s) of a witness or two (also telepathy)? The information, in other words, was accurate, but the mode of communication is in question (from viewing the event—clairvoyance—or from receiving information from the mind(s) of person(s) present—telepathy—or even both?). To add to the confusion, could I not have tapped into the news coverage I would watch after I woke up? In other words, could it have been a precognitive dream, not even real-time psi?

Does it really matter which, as long as the information works? That's the real question, as the words we use to categorize experiences and abilities we call telepathy or clairvoyance or even precognition are just arbitrary in the grand scheme of things.

You make use of the information or not. If not, what good is it? Labels and categories can easily confuse the greater issue of "is the information valuable and usable?" since we can get so wrapped up in classifications such as "remote viewing" that we forget to apply the messages received. Here's an interesting (though sad) dream:

*Often I have dreams and don't realize their significance un-
til the actual event takes place. In one case, I saw an entire
murder take place. I described the house and clothing of the
victims. The faces were fuzzy, but I later learned my friend
was shot by her husband who also killed himself. I was never
in her house, but described the room down to the detail of a
bloody mirror.*

—B. R., New Jersey

The above dream is a good example of how the time factor leaves
you in the cold in trying to determine just what kind of psychic
dream this was. The murder could have occurred at the same
time as the dream, earlier, or later. B. R., not knowing that the
dream was truly significant, would not have tried to deal with
whether the dream occurred at the same time, or before, or after.
B. R. did not even determine just where the event dreamed about
could have occurred, because of incomplete information.

Such dreams can make us feel incomplete, because of the nagging feeling that we should have been able to do something. This
is not always the case. If the dream occurs at the same time as the
event, or the event happens during the sleep period in which the
dream occurs, there is nothing to be done, except perhaps reveal
the dreamed information to interested parties who might be able
to make use of it. For example:

*I dreamed that my brother was down in a deep hole reach-
ing for my help. I tried to help him, but before I could, I woke
up. The next morning I felt very strange and disturbed about
the dream. I told my wife that Bill was in an accident and
was hurt very badly.*

> *About noon, my mother and sister came by with the news*
> *that Bill was in a serious accident and was all broken up. The*
> *truck in which he was riding (in the back) got hit in the back*
> *by a tractor-trailer carrying logs. The accident happened on*
> *a bridge just before the river, and Bill was thrown down an*
> *embankment some fifty feet below the highway.*
>
> *Eight people were in the back of the covered pickup. One*
> *was killed, and my brother was the most seriously injured.*
> —M. T., Virginia

Dreams like this one might also hold a bit of helpful information. There have, in the past, been reports of people who have been hurt in accidents yet not found at the scene of the accident. Dreams of accident sites can be carriers of life-saving information if the dreamer (or someone told about the dream) can use that dreamed information to rescue the injured party. Psychics have had experiences in being able to find lost and injured people, and this information can be provided to psychics and to us normal folks in or out of the dream state.

Record Your Dreams

Keeping track of your dreams to help determine which are psychic and which are not, as well as timing patterns, is a basic first step to possibly doing something with the information. In chapter 13, I'll discuss working with your dreams in depth, but for the moment, here's where to start.

Keep a dream log or journal. As you recall dreams, write them down or audio record them. Some people keep a voice recorder next to their beds or use smartphone apps, others simply a pad and pen. The time we best remember dreams is just as we wake up. Granted, it isn't easy to be awake enough to take down any information, yet not awake enough to have forgotten what you dreamed (just waking up can be an ordeal in itself, as I am well aware). Record or take notes on the dream, especially anything special that seems different than other dreams. Might it be related to a real event?

Make sure you include the date and even the time you woke up remembering the dream. Then, as you learn of events that have an apparent relationship to what you dreamed about, go back over that dream and note which of the contents of the dream were actually related to the events. Note also the timing of the event, and see how that relates to the timing of the dream.

Potential for Real-Time Psi

If you can only connect the dream to the event within the time span of your sleep that night, don't place too much weight on it being precognitive or clairvoyant. Remember, a real-time clairvoyant dream is just as interesting as a precognitive one, even though there's not much you can do to affect an event that has already occurred. The information provided by the dream could shed quite a bit of light on the event itself, helping you intellectually understand what happened or helping you emotionally deal with the consequences of that event or even providing useful information for follow-up.

Awareness of real-time situations, from the rescue and crime scenarios to perceptions of design flaws in products (and perhaps in buildings) are used today, though information is gathered through the use of the normal perceptions and through technological means. Add to the ways we collect such information normally, any new information we might gather instantly (at the time or shortly after the event or inspection) that we might otherwise not get so immediately (or perhaps ever), and we have greater efficiency in saving lives, preventing tragedy, keeping quality control where otherwise there might be little, and helping people understand the circumstances around them that affect them both physically and psychologically.

The potential for real-time psi is incredible. I should mention that there is a potential danger as well. If you have such an experience of receiving information that you connect to a real-time event, there is always the possibility that you are wrong about it. Time can therefore be wasted in trying to do something about an event that hasn't actually happened. Or the information could be incomplete so that it is severely misinterpreted, putting you on to the wrong place or the wrong situation. Or the information is correct but is not actually psychic. It is possible that what you perceived in or out of that dream was a situation that you knew about purely by coincidence. There's always the possibility that information already in your memory about that event (that it was going to happen) was buried deep enough that you didn't know you already knew it.

On an absolute level, we can never be 100 percent sure that a dream was psychic, that it wasn't intuitive leaps of logic using half-memories or deeply buried ones, or that it wasn't coincidence. You can, however, be closer to an assumption that it was information beyond normal perceptions or buried memory if the event you perceive is one removed from your own experience.

What Do We Do with the Details?

A good deal of time, reported experiences lack enough detail or description of a real-time event to be able to connect the information from that experience to one particular event. Lack of detail is the bane of a psychic's existence (and a parapsychologist's as well). I could dream about a real murder occurring and get a clear view of the murderer, but nothing else. I could be absolutely positive that the dream was real. Unfortunately, knowing what a killer looks like without being able to tie him or her to a location somewhere in the world or to a particular murder means that the information is virtually useless. Unless, of course, I were to run into that person sometime in my life. In that case, if I really felt my dream was a true representation of this person now in front of me, that she/he was a murderer, I'd use that information as advice that I should steer clear of this person. I simply do not have enough information to do anything.

In such situations, people who have the experiences need to understand that there may be absolutely nothing to be done with that experience or information. This can be extremely frustrating, and people can even become obsessed with such an experience. It is important to "let it go" rather than feel "I should have done something about it." Better to think that when you see an actual crime being committed, where there is something you can do (like report it to the police, testify, and so on—but be cautious they don't think you had something to do with the crime). Psychics report that they have to "get used to" not being able to do something with all the information they get, just as we all have to do on a daily basis.

One other point to remember is that no matter how clear such experiences might be, how detailed they are, when the info comes to you in a dream, you may have to look carefully at that dream. Imagery from your subconscious might very well be mixed in with the clairvoyant (or other psychic) information. In addition, as with any psychic experience, in life or in a laboratory, it is important to not read too deeply into the picture.

If you dream of a tall, cylindrical, pointed shape, you might try to identify it with a landmark you've seen before, or your subconscious might fill in missing details so that an incomplete, vague shape now looks more like the Eiffel Tower. This often creates a real problem, since that shape may be accurate, but the identification is not. It wasn't the Eiffel Tower, but a tall salt or pepper shaker.

Point of view can distort what we get out of these experiences. We're used to seeing with our eyes, and we've learned to see things proportionally. However, if a shape or an image appears in a dream without anything near it to provide a frame of reference, a tall, pointed, saltshaker floating on a background field of a solid color might actually look bigger than it is. Or part of a car might not look like part of a car, because the image fills your whole field of mental vision.

You simply need to be aware that the imagery or information coming through on such channels can be incomplete or provided from a different frame of reference. If you feel that information coming through in a dream or psychic vision is truly psychic, try to look at it as just a few pieces of a puzzle laid on a big piece of white paper. If you can piece together the puzzle, great. If not, then the pieces might fit with what you already know about a dozen different situations. Figuring which of those situations is the right one may be difficult if you try to think about it too much. You might simply go with your hunches or feelings as to how this information relates to reality. With that, you might find greater relevance of that dreamed information to your life.

Real Problems Caused by Psychic Dreams

Running your life solely on the basis of what these dreams or waking experiences seem to tell you may leave you unconnected with the real world. Pay attention to what's really going on around you (stay grounded, to put it another way).

Clairvoyant and precognitive dreams can cause problems in other ways. There have been a few cases that have made it to court of someone dreaming of a murder. Feeling civic-minded, the dreamer reports the dream, which came with very detailed information, to the police. For want of a better suspect, the dreamer is arrested, the police viewing the dream as a kind of confession to the crime. In some instances, such reports really do turn out to be confessions—in some cases the dreamer really is the killer. But in other cases, the dreamer was an innocent bystander, someone who somehow knew about the incident. In those cases, the police have little or no evidence that could even be stretched to cover the dreamer. In a couple of cases, however, the fact that the dreamer was the only suspect (simply because of an attitude of "She/he had to have done it. How else could she/he have known so much about it?") was enough to hold the dreamer for trial.

Dreams of such detail are generally rare. Police typically have to find hard evidence upon which to build a case before following through on arresting someone who had a dream. They're more likely to believe the dreamer was an eyewitness and proceed from there. In fact, there are cases on record where a witness to a crime or situation later comes forward and admits that what was seen was actually from a dream, rather than physical perception.

In addition, there are police departments and individual officers and detectives who have worked with psychics on criminal cases, which indicates an openness to such experiences, as the dream of an average person being possibly psychic rather than an indicator that the dreamer had something to do with the crime. Also consider that *psychic* may not be a word in the vocabulary of the people you report the information to. If you do report such information anonymously, you may also have to contend with how to present it. "I dreamed about a murder" will probably be less accepted than "I have information relating to a murder."

Therein, again, lies the problem of packaging psychic information, whether clairvoyant, precognitive, or of other forms. Our society in the western hemisphere says that these experiences are not normal. Therefore, to get the information across to the people who need to know, you sometimes have to rephrase the way you want to talk about it.

Real-time psi perceptions of events apparently occur in our lives, regardless of whether we consider ourselves psychic or not. Many immediately label them with the word *coincidence* or the phrase "lucky guess." Others assume that all similar experiences, psychic or not when you look carefully at them, are psychic. We can go to extremes in either direction. What's important to remember is that the information coming to our conscious minds from dreams, from memory, psychically or not, is being flagged as important. Paying attention to it may provide solutions to problems in our lives. Dismissing the experiences as invalid information because the vehicle of the information, an apparently psychic dream or waking experience, is not considered normal or even possible, by some, is to do ourselves a great injustice.

Psychic Dreams as "News Reports"

The majority of people who have dreams we can classify as clairvoyant or real-time psychic dreams, have dreams a lot less exciting than those that might deal with murder or other crimes, or even those that deal with disasters happening in the here and now. Most reported clairvoyant dreams (and waking clairvoyance experiences) tend to have to do with our own lives or the lives of those in our immediate range of experience. By that I mean relatives, friends, or people we know quite a bit about (such as political figures, people prevalent in sports or entertainment, or locals we know about but may not know personally). Clairvoyant dreams can be quite unsatisfying, since unless there's something we can do about the situation we see in our dreams, we might as well be watching a news report on TV or reading an account in the newspaper.

That, of course, may be the very reason our minds bring in the information: as a simple news report. We seek out news on the web or watch/listen to TV/radio news (or perhaps still read the newspaper) because we have curiosity or fears about the world around us and the immediate events and people that may affect our lives. Such dreams and experiences may be very satisfying for that reason, allowing us to know about events as they are happening rather than having to wait for the actual report in the news.

If your experience in or out of dreams says "Here's something that's happening right now, or just happened," follow up on it, within reason. See if it happened and think about how such information may affect your own life, or the lives of those around you.

You may be surprised at just how much you're really connecting with the world around you. Or you may learn that the psychic/clairvoyant part of you is simply very good at keeping you abreast of local, national, and world events happening in the now.

As for the future, that's coming up next....

chapter 10

Future Dreaming: Precognition

Humans are planners. Every day many people consult an oracle of sorts who provides information that may affect what they wear, what they carry, and even their travel plans. The oracle predicts things for the whole day and for days to come, yet is often quite wrong—especially the further out the prediction is from the event itself. This oracle is mainstream and often trained in a physical science.

I'm talking about the weather person and weather service, though from the above, I might as well be talking about some psychic. In the psychic world, we consider whether information can come to us from a future—either one that is predetermined or one that is probable. In the world of meteorologists, the predictions are based on models of the behavior of the weather, the models themselves based on observation and analysis of current and past conditions. Can information travel from the future to the present, or is it all guesswork or something similar to what meteorologists do?

Cause and Effect

We usually think in terms of cause and effect with regard to things happening, where the event (the cause) brings about a particular happening or outcome (the effect). With precognition, it is suggested that the effect (the precognitive experience) *precedes* the cause (the predicted event in the future).

Abraham Lincoln had a dream. In his dream, he found himself walking through the halls of the White House. He came upon mourners and a funeral. When he asked "Who is dead in the White House?" the reply was "The president … he was killed by an assassin." This occurred in March 1865. In April, this dream, which he had discussed with several people, came true—Abraham Lincoln was dead, killed by assassin John Wilkes Booth. The indication of Lincoln's death came *before* the cause, the assassination.

Wanting to Know the Future

Since the time humankind could think and develop our own rituals, religions, and explanations for the way the universe works, we have been interested in, if not obsessed with, the notion that some specially gifted people have access to the future. Divination techniques to know the future run a wide gamut from utilizing the movement of the stars to studying rune stones, from watching the flights of birds or migration patterns of animals to reading animal entrails, from throwing sticks to staring into a crystal ball. But all of these require special talents or learned skills.

Everyone dreams, and so the future as it appears in the dreams of everyday folk is more accessible to us all. While it is true that some cultures may raise certain individuals above others for more frequent dreams of future events, we all seem capable of somehow receiving information across time, whether in the dream state or simply through hunches, intuitive flashes, or so-called visions.

Precognition vs. PK in Testing

Precognition as a studied ability in parapsychological research is not difficult to test. You set up an experiment for which the target has not yet been selected. Your participant makes a selection or prediction and *then* you use a random process or device to select the target. You check to see if the target matches the prediction.

Sounds easy, but there are inherent problems. One is whether we are using precognition to see the future or psychokinesis (PK) to influence the future, in this case potentially influencing the process used to select the target so the correct one is chosen. From the philosophical and physical end we have the question of how it's possible to gain information across time, and even whether there is a definite future for us to access.

Ultimately, if one accepts the existence of PK (and some of my colleagues do not), we can't know for sure that PK is or isn't happening in a given experiment. Even if you check for this ability, giving the same person a PK test before the precognition experiment and that person does well, there's no way to tell whether PK has or has not influenced the machine in the specific precognition experiment. We have no detection devices to look for PK as yet. There is also the added (and dreaded) possibility that the experimenter, wishing for certain results, uses his or her own PK to cause the participant's test results to be a certain way.

Of course, there are enough stories about people *knowing* future events that precognition is at least a possibility, and today there are parapsychologists and others who have concluded that precognition can account for all of ESP (and even some other reported phenomena/abilities like evidential mediumship). The spontaneous precognition reports support the idea that the precognition experiments are more than relevant, that they don't have to be psychokinetic.

Additionally, the reverse may be true: precognition of a slightly nonrandom bunch of targets may simulate psychokinesis. Even with a random event generator, there are times that the output may be less random (more heads than tails in flips of a coin)—sort of like some nice runs of good luck. If you knew when to start, when the run of less random targets began, it might look like you were influencing the outcomes. Instead of influencing the output of the REG, you are using precognition to choose just when to press the start button to begin the test (which is when that run of less random targets starts), not when to actually start influencing the machine. This is called Decision Augmentation Theory.

Let's say you went to a casino and decided to play the slots. With psychokinetic ability, you might be able to influence the slot machines to pay off, to come up with the right results after pulling the lever. On the other hand, you might roam around the casino until your precognition told you that a certain machine would pay off after three more pulls. Knowing this, you know just *when* to try each of the machines so that they pay off.

The issue of psychokinesis (creating the future) vs. precognition (knowing the future) is significantly less serious in dreams.

Time Itself

J. W. Dunne, with his extensive study of his own dreams written up in his 1927 book *An Experiment with Time (reprinted in 2001),* began looking for dreams that truly provided evidence of precognitive information in normal dream states. Until then, other researchers had asked the public for dreams and other experiences that might be subjected to analysis for psychic correlations, but Dunne went a step further in taking a pool of his own dreams rather than a grouping of the experiences of others. Dunne is to be commended for this, according to playwright and writer J. B. Priestly in *Man & Time,* and for bringing dreams and the act of remembering, recording, and analyzing one's own dreams into focus for the general public.

The other contribution of Dunne in that book and later ones, including *The Serial Universe,* deals with time itself, as he extensively explored ideas of the structure of time and its relation to space.

There has been much discussion of the idea of time itself in physics, philosophy, and even psychology. There are only *some* things we know about the way it (probably) works, and there's no real agreement as to what time is and whether it even exists or whether it's merely a construct of consciousness. There are numerous books on the subject to be found via online booksellers and your public library, and I highly recommend you consider reading those that offer conflicting opinions to get a better understanding of the problem of time. You might also read lots of science fiction, especially time travel novels, or those dealing with the structure of time. One science fiction novel I highly recommend is *Jack of Eagles* by James Blish, as it deals with the ideas of J. W. Dunne.

Mutable Time

Time is changeable. We know this from two areas of science— physics and psychology. Albert Einstein dealt with the concept of time dilation as part of relativity, a concept proven by experimentation. Time dilation deals with both rate of time passing as well as how fast one moves through space. The faster you go (in relation to the rest of the universe), the slower time proceeds for you.

For example, if someone were to travel in a spacecraft close to the speed of light, and take a grand tour of our solar system, depending on how far one traveled, you could return in a few months or a couple of years, as far as the people you left behind were concerned. To you, traveling near the speed of light, perhaps a few days would have passed. Time would proceed at its normal pace here on Earth, while on the ship, it would slow to a crawl. And since time itself slows for the ship, so does perception of time. You would not even notice how or if time has changed until you stepped off the spacecraft back on Earth. Your watch/ calendar would say that a few days had gone by, while the calendar on Earth would say differently.

What this means is that time's passage can be physically slowed down or even sped up. Time is not a steady, straight arrow thing. It is really only our Western cultural concept that time flows into the future on a straight path at a steady rate, not actual reality. The more you hear or read about time as a concept, the more confused you might get, as you learn that the more you study time, the less you realize you know. This doesn't say that we can get information from the future, merely that time is not a constant.

Others in the physical sciences have suggested that there is no time; that what measurements we make are artificial, a function of our consciousness and ability to interact with the world around us. Still another concept is that of simultaneous time—that past, present, and future all exist, and it's only our attention that says we are in the present.

Subjective Time

Psychologists have learned that one can change a person's perception of time. Experiments with people isolated from time-keeping devices, including the rising and setting of the sun, have shown that even the person's body clock, which is basically on a twenty-four-hour cycle, can be affected, and can change by even tens of hours without discomfort.

Linear Time: Is There a Future?

We seem to know there's a past (we've been there) and a present (we're there now), but a future? We never really get there, since as we progress through time, our present becomes the past, and the future becomes the present.

One major concept is that time and destiny are one and the same—we are predestined to live our lives in a particular way; the future is already written in stone. If there is an objective future already laid out for us, maybe it is possible to somehow reach into it and see the specifics of tomorrow or next month. However, this appears to remove all free will and decision-making power from us. If we are destined to do a particular thing tomorrow, whether we like it or not, then we are merely puppets of some universal puppeteer, characters in the Book of Life. Maybe we could flip through the pages ahead to the ending of our particular story as our own awareness of the present shifts from one page to the next.

Unfortunately, if we get information from an inevitable future, one question comes up: What good is it? If I see I'm to die tomorrow, and I know I can't change that, what's the point?

Predestination is an idea that many have a hard time accepting, especially scientists dealing with time and with subatomic physics.

In quantum physics, in the reality below the level of atom-sized particles, the world works more in probabilities than definites. We don't know the outcome to some event until there is an observer there to witness the outcome.

Probabilities

The idea of probable futures appeals to many, myself included. This is the concept that there are a few, perhaps many, future paths likely to occur, depending on certain events or decisions happening in the present. If you've seen *Back to the Future,* and especially *Back to the Future II* and *Back to the Future III,* or read time travel science fiction (or DC or Marvel Comics), or are a fan of *Doctor Who* or *Star Trek* (any of the series), you are probably familiar with the idea of going back in time and doing something that changes the future.

In *Back to the Future,* Marty McFly (Michael J. Fox) accidentally changes the past, then has to rectify the error. If his parents don't fall in love, he's not going to be born. During the fix, George McFly (Marty's dad) hauls off and hits Biff, the town bully. When Marty returns to 1985, his father is no longer a wimp—he's a successful science fiction writer. And by warning Doc Brown (the scientist who invents the time machine, played by Christopher Lloyd), Marty enables that character to have the foreknowledge to wear a bulletproof vest on a particular night in 1985, thereby saving his life.

Back to the Future II seemed, to many, a bit confusing to follow, as Marty McFly and company deal with major changes and alternating timelines thanks to a little more time tampering. Marty heads off into the future to help his kids, only to find that an almanac of sports scores gets sent back to 1955 to Biff, who proceeds to make himself rich based on the information in the almanac (knowing all the sports scores for the coming fifty or so years gave him a distinct advantage when gambling). This sets off a chain of events that alters Marty's timeline, sending him and Doc Brown back again to 1955, where he (and the audience) gets to watch himself on his first visit to the 50s. Sound confusing?

Well, luckily, all is fixed in *Back to the Future III*. Marty McFly gets a chance to go back further into the past where he rescues Doc Brown from a future in which he's gunned down by (who else?) the town bully, an ancestor of Biff's. By the end of the film, all is right with the timestream, although the present Marty returns to is (fortunately for him) the happier one with his folks being successful. More importantly, we see that Marty has learned from his experiences and is able to make a choice about his own future based on what he learned in his time travels. The choice is one that will keep him whole and happy.

One reviewer of *Back to the Future III* seemed to have a problem with the timestream changing as it did. The stimulus prompting Marty to go back to the Old West to rescue Doc is a tombstone indicating that he died in a gunfight shortly after arriving there. Marty changes things when he goes back to 1885, and the tombstone vanishes. The reviewer found major fault with that—how could Doc Brown die before the time machine was even invented?

Changing Timelines

A third season episode of *Star Trek: The Next Generation* ("Yesterday's *Enterprise*," 1990) also dealt with a change in time. A previous incarnation of the starship *Enterprise* escapes a battle with the Romulans through a time warp, bringing it twenty-two years into its future (to the time of Captain Picard's *Enterprise)*. This disappearance of a Federation vessel from a crucial point in time changes things. The Federation is, from the perspective of the viewer, suddenly at war with the Klingons, a dead crew member suddenly lives (Tasha Yar, security chief), and others are no longer aboard (Worf, who, as a Klingon, would now be at war with the Federation).

It is only through the urging of the character Guinan (Whoopi Goldberg) that the other *Enterprise* is sent back to rectify things. In fact, if not for Guinan's recognition that "something's not right" with their time, that there'd been a change of some kind, the new *Enterprise* would have been destroyed by Klingons. Apparently, Guinan's race of beings is sensitive to time, and therefore to any changes in it. Why did no one else notice? Because if there were a change in the past, everything from that point forward, including all memory of everyone who lived at that point and after, would be dependent on the time-altering event and what came after for facts. New timeline ... new events ... new memories.

The time-traveling *Doctor Who* often deals with issues of avoiding changes in the timestream, even when his human companions would love to do otherwise. The Doctor doesn't like mucking about with changing the way things were, which for him could be all of time, given his travels to the far past and far future. He speaks of that possibility, how dangerous his people (the Time Lords) have figured it out to be, and how there are some points in time (and space) that cannot be changed, no matter how much one tries to interfere.

All this, of course, is science fiction.

Can We Change the Future?

If we knew of something supposed to happen tomorrow that didn't quite suit us, we might do something to prevent it. If the event then doesn't happen, we're happy. We may make a guess about what is likely to happen tomorrow when we go to work and then make a decision to change our own behaviors to create a less likely outcome. The future that would *probably* happen doesn't.

Perhaps precognition is like weather prediction, our minds telling us what is *probably* going to happen in the future, given what we know now. Our brains become computers, calculating the odds of certain events happening in the future given what's been happening in the present and what's happened in the past. We make a prediction of that probable future. If it doesn't happen because of chance or because someone made a non-probable decision or because some unknown person or event was left out of the calculations, our prediction fails. If we move to prevent the prediction from coming true, that future never comes about.

We may be using clairvoyant ability to gather more information about things happening in the present, so that our brains have more data to make an educated guess of the future. Once again, though, that probable future is just that: *probable*, not definite. When it doesn't happen for the reasons named above, the prediction is invalid, no matter how good the guess was. Human decision-making can cause such probabilities to change at a moment's notice.

Let's assume there is some kind of objective future, and that it is changeable ("Always in motion is the future," to quote Yoda from *The Empire Strikes Back*). Perhaps precognitive experience, assuming psi abilities work at all, is an awareness of the future *most likely to occur.* When a prediction is made, then actions change (either because of the prediction or other factors that show up later), the probability changes and another future, another outcome becomes "most likely."

The Intervention Paradox

This brings up the idea of the intervention paradox, which looks at altering outcomes of events perceived by precognition. Think about this: I have a precognitive experience during which I see myself in a car accident at a certain intersection tomorrow when a car runs a red light. I decide not to drive at all, and to stay away from that intersection in general. The next evening, I hear about a car running a red light at that intersection, narrowly missing a bus. I also learn that the time it happened was about the time I would regularly drive through the intersection. The event happens, though not as predicted. No accident, especially not one with me involved.

I intervened in my daily routine because of that prediction. The information came to me from the future, yet by acting on that information, I avoided that future all together. By intervening, I caused a time paradox: How could I get information from a future that never comes to be? There's an effect (the psychic experience) without a cause (the accident).

Another example: Let's say the president of the United States is told that there is to be an assassination attempt on his life on a particular day, and that the psychic who saw this attempt also saw the president die. Perhaps that particular president decides to listen, and he wears a bulletproof vest that day (and puts more Secret Service folks on the job). The assassin attempts to get near the president, but he is scared off by the extra security. The assassin, a suspicious-looking individual, is noticed by a Secret Service agent, who stops him, frisks him, finds the gun, and arrests him. No attempt, no death, yet a real threat that could have happened.

Intervention due to the extra information not only saved the president, but also changed the psychic's vision of the way the future was to go. Some would say the psychic was wrong, others would say the psychic enabled the Secret Service to change the flow of events, which became the *most likely* future.

Of course, the psychic's prediction may have resulted from the psychic somehow telepathically picking up the intent to assassinate the president from the mind of the assassin, as well as the assassin's plans to try it on a certain day at a certain location. It is not always necessary to say the information comes from the future. It may be extra information from the here and now.

Backward in Time

According to some physicists, one major interpretation of quantum mechanics is that at that level of size reality there is no barrier to information traveling both directions in time. Some physicists have postulated that antiparticles, such as positrons (an electron with a positive, rather than a negative, charge), are actually particles traveling backward in time, which is why their charges look opposite to what we'd expect. Whether these particles can actually carry information to a human mind is a whole different question.

Can the future actually affect the present or the past? We really don't know for sure. That's unfortunately the best answer I can give, although many will offer more definite answers (especially many self-professed psychics). It appears that sometimes there is information about the future that shows up unannounced and this information comes true. Sometimes that information can be used to make other choices and to effectively alter that envisioned future. Of course, there is also the aspect of coincidence to consider, though the role of that in a given, apparent precognitive experience is difficult, if not impossible to assess.

When one has a psychic flash or vision or gut feeling about the future, the information content varies from simply a feeling that something (good or bad) is about to happen to a clear picture/message of what is going to happen. Knowledge of a future being spotty may mean not being able to directly connect the partial information or sensation to the event until after the event happens. Of course at that point there's not a lot you can do to affect that event. Specific information about a future event, when it is recognized as such, can be helpful. But first the experient must decide that the information is about a future event and that the information *can* be utilized at all.

If the experient believes in an inevitable future, he may do nothing but wait it out. On the other hand, even a helpful psychic who knows to use precognitive information can't be too helpful without specifics.

People have had precognitive experiences about all sorts of disasters. If an individual got information that a DC-10 was going to crash tomorrow in Chicago, even with enough detail as to what was wrong with the plane, that doesn't mean anything can be done. Without airline information, and considering the hundreds of flights going in and out of O'Hare airport on a given day, it would be next to impossible to figure out just which flight to ground. Incomplete information can be extremely frustrating in this respect.

Precognitive Dreaming

There is the added complication of dream imagery that could effectively confound or confuse the identification of precognitive information. Not only is there the difficult process of remembering the fine details of a dream, but also the problem of separating out from a dream just what is psychic information and what has been added by the subconscious to make the dream more interesting.

Nancy Sondow, in the January 1988 issue of *the Journal of the American Society for Psychical Research* ("The Decline of Precognized Events with the Passage of Time: Evidence from Spontaneous Dreams"), re-created J. W. Dunne's precognition experiment with her own dreams. In the article, she discussed a finding of her experiment that coincided with that of other precognitive studies and observations of spontaneous precognitive experiences. She found that most of her dreams that could have been considered precognitive came true within a day of the dream. There tends to be a falling off of how accurate the premonitions are the further down the line into the future the events are. Sondow brings up the point that if what we are reading of the future comes from the branching of possible futures, the further into the future one tries to see, the more likelihood that you could be picking up on the wrong branch. It's kind of like predicting the weather.

She also discussed a couple of objections to any analysis of spontaneous dream precognitions that can affect the drop-off rate. Given all the possible things one might dream about, if you wait long enough and wade through enough dreams, the dreamed event may happen, or a real event will merely be connected to the dreamed event by the person doing the analysis. If I predict that I will someday soon come into some money, one might connect that prediction to anything from my receiving a bonus at work (which I expected anyway) to finding a coin or dollar bill lying in the street. Coincidence, two events related to one another by an observer, is responsible if you wait long enough. So, if the event dreamed about happens very soon after the dream, there is much less chance that the dream connection to the event was coincidence.

The other objection is one she calls the "memory-artifact interpretation," which has to do with the length of time since a dream occurred and the decay of memory (forgetting) of details that might otherwise be connected as precognized bits of information. The longer you wait for the event to occur, the better the chance that you'll forget some details that might allow you to connect the dream to the actual event.

Of course, there are some features of precognitive and psychic dreams in general that often set them apart from other kinds of dreams. One is the quality of the dream imagery, which might be more vivid and evocative that other dreams. You remember it more clearly and somehow just *know* it relates to real events. The other is a feeling that occurs for people when they come to the event earlier dreamed about, a sense of déjà vu, that the event is truly familiar because they dreamed about it.

Besides the fall-off due to attempts at picking out the correct future branch, Sondow also discusses the idea that there may be this decline in precognition due to the way we deal with the future. The immediate future tends to be more important to us than a time further down the road. Therefore, this immediate future, which is also less subject to extensive branching off, may be better and more frequently targeted by our psi. Sondow brings in the point, however, that we do sometimes dream of people or events other than ourselves, people and events not as important to us, so this argument may be less effective than a fall-off due to further branching possible futures.

Such precognitive dreams as those of disasters, while not necessarily affecting us directly, may be important to us because of the intensity of the emotions they create. On October 21, 1966, a coal deposit on the side of a mountain in Aberfan, Wales, slid down on top of a schoolhouse. More than one hundred people were killed, mostly children. This event caused a very emotional response in many who heard of it. Before the event, many people apparently felt feelings of dread, of something awful about to happen (precognition). There were similar responses felt at the time of the disaster (clairvoyance). Dr. J. C. Barker, a psychiatrist, solicited dreams about the disaster and found some potentially precognitive ones. These included a report that one of the girls who died in the disaster spoke to her mother about a dream of something that was to happen (and about death) two weeks before the disaster.

Unlike the dream of this little girl, most of the others had no direct connection to the coal accident. The issue of importance seems to hold little weight in light of situations like the Aberfan disaster, or with cases of people dreaming of other such situations that they themselves are not going to be directly involved in. However, the high emotional response of large groups of people to a disaster such as Aberfan, or much more recently to 9/11 as I noted earlier in the book (including my own precognitive pre-reaction), may be what drives the precognitive experience.

Far from all precognitive dreams have to do with disaster or destruction, though due to their high emotional impact, those are most often the ones people take note of. Let's look at a few dream experiences reported to me over the years.

Some Dreams of Illustration

I dreamed about going to buy something in a store, then before making the purchase, discovering that my checkbook was empty. The dream came true the next day.
    —*S. K., Colorado*

The above dream could either be precognitive or simply based on the knowledge that S. K. was planning to shop the next day, and the nonconscious awareness of the emptiness of the checkbook. If S. K. had been the one to tear the last check out, leaving the checkbook empty, that fact could show up as a reminder in a dream. S. K. should have looked in the checkbook before shopping.

I had a dream about my mother's friend. I dreamed that she had on a dark blue T-shirt and she held up a check, saying that she got her income tax refund on a Monday.
    The next day, she went over to my mother's house, had on a navy blue T-shirt, and it was Monday. She had just gotten her income tax check.
    —*L. R., New Hampshire*

This is a very straightforward dream. Unless L. R. knew that the mother's friend was due over to visit and that the friend had been expecting an income tax check to come and that the friend tends to wear navy blue T-shirts (either in general, or specifically on Mondays), then we certainly would judge this precognitive.

These next two dreams are also fairly specific, though in each case, the information is not 100 percent right on all points, a fairly normal occurrence.

I had a very vivid dream of hitting a deer with my car on my
way to mail Mother's Day cards at a post office three towns
away. The next week, in that particular town, I hit a deer
with my car—on Mother's Day.
    —M. A., G. P., New Jersey

The Mother's Day cards (which, I presume, would never be mailed
on Mother's Day) represent the date of the deer accident, rather
than the actuality of mailing the cards. Otherwise, the town and
accident are on point.

I dreamed that a person I didn't know left money to me in a
will, the sum of $22,000 a year for ten years. The next day,
my friend's mother found her deceased husband's will in a
safe, (I never met the husband), and with it a bill of sale
from a ranch he'd sold. My friend's mother was to receive
$22,000 a year for ten years.
    —T. D., Idaho

In T. D.'s dream, a person she didn't know (the deceased man) left
$22,000 for ten years to his living wife in a will. While the money
was not left to T. D., the information otherwise proved true. You
can, however, make a case that this was not a precognitive dream.
Since the will existed in real time, T. D. may have picked up the
information from the will, rather than from the friend's mother's
discovery of the will. That would make this a clairvoyant dream.

About sixteen and a half years ago both my parents died. My
mom, forty-eight years old, died in late January 1973, and
my dad, sixty-four years old, died in early March the same

year. I was twenty-three years old at the time; my brother was twenty-four years old. The death of my parents was a total shock to my relatives and to my brother, who eventually had an emotional breakdown. I, on the other hand, "knew." I had dreams for three months prior to their deaths. I thought I was losing my mind. I cried for three months. I tried to warn my mom "something terrible is going to happen!" When it finally came to pass it was like a rerun of a bad movie. I was now part of the dream and wanted to wake up. I lived through everything that happened.

It was a week before my mother's death that I physically went through her final physical pain. I could not breathe; my dad helped me walk through the long hallway to the front door and opened it. I eventually was able to take deep breaths and it passed. It was a horrible feeling of drowning.

It was a week to that night my mother took the same, painful walk, unable to breathe, her lungs full of water. She never made it to the hospital. She was Dead On Arrival. I had begged my mom to go to the doctor, she was on high blood pressure medication and was careful of her diet. She also had hypertension. The doctor said she had a massive cardiac arrest.

My dad mourned terribly for weeks, crying. He worked long, hard hours. He promised me he would never leave me, but I knew when he left for work that Friday morning it would be the last time I would see him. The night before he was so happy; he had dreamed of my mom. He died on the job—it was a massive heart attack. He collapsed getting off the bulldozer and someone caught him as he fell. The paramedics revived him, he opened his eyes for a brief moment, smiled, and closed them. My cousin told me all this, as he was at the scene, having worked at a firehouse in the area.

When I got his call to come to the hospital I knew! I told my boss that there was no point in going to the hospital because my dad was dead, even though no one told me at the time. I just simply knew.

I was physically fine, but not too sure of reality. I was hoping I would eventually wake up from a horrid dream. The funeral director who took charge of both my parents' wakes took me aside and told me he had never seen the kind of smiles both my parents had when they left this world. His experience with my parents had him amazed, and he actually had to lessen the smiles because it filled their faces.

As they lay in their coffins I knew exactly how they were going to be dressed. I had nothing to do with it, as my mother's sister had bought my mother's final outfit. My mom was dressed in a blue satin dress; my mom did not like blue. I saw this in my dream, even down to the single red rose one of my cousins put on her chest. My dad and I were closer so I did have some say as to what he would have wanted.

My dreams were a scrapbook of some sort. I don't know why I had foreseen all of this. Perhaps it was so I could be prepared. I have lived with guilt and felt that perhaps I had not done enough to alter things. Reading your book has made me feel better coping with my feelings.

—A. N., Brooklyn, NY

One of the key ideas as to why people have precognitive dreams about disastrous events we are unable to change is brought up in the previous letter. "Perhaps it was so I could be prepared," said

A. N. The idea that such an experience can prepare us to better cope with grief has also been connected with sightings of apparitions of relatives and friends who have just died. We become aware of the death somehow before the normal means of communication are used to advise us of the events so we can be psychologically prepared to deal with that forthcoming knowledge.

A. N. attempted to get her mother to go to a doctor before she died. The warning was not heeded, but that is to be expected. Most people would not base their next movements on information presented to them from someone else's dream. However, it makes good sense that when someone tells you that an illness or a medical problem is going to get worse, if you in fact are not feeling up to normal or you already know you're a "little ill," to go to the doctor to get yourself checked out. This makes good sense whether the person telling you to do so had a dream or not.

> *I had a dream that my sister went for a long drive. While she was driving, her car began to swerve all over the road. She lost control and went off a cliff. I could see that her front tires had metal sticking through the rubber.*
>
> *When I told her of my dream, she remembered that some of my other dreams had come true. She took her car to a gas station and found out that the steel belts in her tires were broken and coming through the rubber.*
>
> —*E. R., Alaska*

The above dream is an example of one that is heeded, having a direct effect on the future perceived. There was a real problem with the tires. E. R. perceived that the future, with those tire problems, could cause dire consequences for the sister. Luckily, the sister heeded the dream and headed for a gas station (maybe just to be on the safe side). Did it hurt anybody to check out the tires? No. Even if there'd been nothing wrong, having tires checked is an easy thing to do. In this case, it presumably saved a life.

Once again we can look at the source of the information: Did E. R. gain the insight of the accident directly from the future or was it a real-time psychic perception of the problems with the tires (plus a little supposition that such problems with tires would lead to an accident)? This does not really matter unless you're a parapsychologist going crazy trying to figure all this stuff out.

Here are a couple of experiences where the premonitions were heeded and changes in predicted futures made. The first is a precognitive dream experience, the second a "feeling" that something was to happen. Both come from the personal experiences of Joanne Mied of Psychogenic Solutions in Novato, California.

Once I was working at a resort and dreamed that one of the older buildings caught on fire. Interestingly enough, when the staff was alerted, two other people reported dreams of fires in the resort buildings within the preceding days. The fire extinguishers were serviced and the staff was given fire safety and firefighting instructions. When a small fire did break out, it was quickly extinguished by the person in the area at that time.

My husband and a few other adults were responsible for a dozen teenagers on a trip to Hawaii several years ago. When we went to the beach it was our policy to post one of the men as a lifeguard. One day I had a feeling that one of the children would drown. I told my husband, so he posted an additional guard and they moved closer to the surf and

refrained from conversation. Sure enough, an hour later, one
of the teenagers, Joe, got caught in a serious undertow, but
because his predicament was noted early, the guards were
able to give him instructions and help him to safety.
  —*Joanne Mied, Novato, CA*

Precognitive experiences, whether in dreams or in our waking states, can spur us on to action if we pay attention to them. The main problem of acting on the information can be illustrated by the next dream, which is similar, in that a warning may have prevented a terrible accident from happening.

In high school, at age 17, I had a friend named Dana. She
had relatives in Nevada whom she visited several times a
year. I had a dream one night that she was driving to Reno
and had a terrible accident and died.

The next day I asked her if she had any plans to go to
Reno soon. She looked at me strangely and said, yes, she was
going that weekend. I told her about my dream, and an-
other friend there turned white and said she'd had the same
dream. Neither of us, who are still friends, are pranksters.

Dana told us we had vivid imaginations and that she
was still going. However, she later decided not to go and is
still with us.

That dream was like no other I've ever had. I really be-
lieve she's alive today because she did not go.
  —*F. C., California*

This is a situation where the future, had it really been that Dana was to die if she went to Reno, is impossible to judge. Dana decided, for whatever reason, not to go to Reno. Whether that had anything to do with the dream warnings of the other two girls or not is impossible to say. Whether Dana was correct in saying that they had vivid imaginations is also impossible to say. Since she didn't go, there was no accident or death.

Was this a precognitive dream experience? Since we don't really know (nor can we ever know) what would have happened if Dana had gone to Reno, that question cannot be answered.

A friend of mine had broken his leg; he was in a cast for five weeks. I was absent from our class the sixth week. I dreamed he had no cast in choir class and that I walked up to him and said "I knew you had your cast off." Two days later, everything went right into place, and I saw he had no cast. I went to him, repeated the words I had said in my dream, adding that I had dreamed this would happen. He moved away from me like I had some sort of plague.

—C. K., New Jersey

In the events that followed this dream, it would appear that C. K. purposely followed up on the dream with the same words uttered in that dream. The reaction? Typical... the friend thought C. K. was weird or "had some sort of plague." Sadly, this is the reaction of many people when friends relate psychic experiences. Rather than accepting the experiences for what they are, or even trying to look for alternate experiences, most of us react from either fear or the idea that such experiences are not normal. In fact, subjective paranormal experiences like this one are quite normal, and would undoubtedly be considered such if everyone came out publicly with their experiences, rather than keeping them inside due to the assumption (though often correct) that people will think they're nuts.

Of course, there is an alternate explanation for C. K.'s dream: C. K., knowing that the cast would inevitably come off and that choir class was inevitable with the friend, simply had a dream about that anticipated class. It is logical, even down to a point of C. K. possibly anticipating in the dream that the friend would react negatively if approached with a psychic experience.

> *My dream states are not quite clear and are usually dan-*
> *ger signals about someone not present. The unusual thing is*
> *that the person closest to the one endangered appears, rather*
> *than the person involved. For example, my uncle appeared*
> *to me in July warning of my aunt's heart attack in Septem-*
> *ber, even giving the month. I contacted my mother about it.*
>
> *Then I saw Bob Hope appear three months before Bing*
> *Crosby's death.*
> *—M. A., California*

Here we have a fairly common problem with psychic dreams. M. A., like many others, has dreams of future events in which there are symbolic representations of individuals affected, in this case the perceived "person closest to the one endangered." In the dreams of others, symbols may represent people or even specifics of the situations. It is interesting that the dreamer comes to recognize the symbol as such and can decipher what that symbol represents.

In various methods of working with dreams, the dreamworker may help people come to terms with their own internal symbology and mythology, rather than having the dreamer become dependent on someone else's symbology (as with most of those dream interpretation books out there).

In M. A.'s dreams, there appears to be a conscious recognition of the symbols in advance of the actual events occurring. I have received other similar reports, such as one that came from a San Francisco Bay Area woman who felt she was having precognitive dreams. She'd had a dream of a black milk truck, which was followed (after some days) by a relative killed in collision with a truck. It's hard to say that the dream truck representative of the actual event, since there was little in advance of the relative's death to tie that dream symbol to anyone's death in particular. It is possible that the dream was representative of something else. Without a better look at the woman's dreams in general, a connection between that event and the symbol that happened after the event, is a tenuous one; and even then it wasn't very clear.

The woman's question to me was not whether that had been a psychic experience (for she accepted it as such), but what she could do about future events if she continues to have such dreams.

Of course, unless you recognize the dream as providing information about a future event, and unless you can decipher what the symbols represent, there's not a whole lot you can do with that information. It's too incomplete and not even something you are going to consciously associate with a future event. You really can't do something about a situation if you have no information other than "something bad happened in my dream," and you can't feel guilty that you "should have done something" when, after the fact, you connect a dream to an event.

Sometimes, there is not even so much as a memory that you had a dream about a future event, until the event happens, as with this next experience.

> *The first time visiting a friend in Chicago, I had an experience. We were taking a shortcut and were about to enter a newly constructed building. Before entering, I hesitated and began to describe the yet-to-be-completed inside. I had dreamed of this place and now it was before me.*
> —J. U., Georgia

As mentioned earlier, one of the more common experiences connected with psi is the feeling you'd been in a situation before, known as *déjà vu*. One of the close to fifty possible explanations for particular déjà vu experiences relates to forgotten dreams: you have that sense of familiarity because at one point in the past you had a dream very similar to (or perhaps exactly like) a situation you're entering into. Rather than remembering a dream at that point, you simply get a strong, but vague, sense of familiarity, of having lived it before.

In my own life, I've had many déjà vu experiences, most of which are simply a strong sense of familiarity. Sometimes I do get the sense that the situation was something I had dreamed about, though I recognize that the dream was only similar to the situation, and I really can't consider that a psychic experience.

On the other hand, as with J. U.'s letter, I have on occasion had the memory of a dream rushing back into my mind as a physical experience is happening. I have an absolute *knowing* (or sensation) that the information rushing in was from a dream, and on some occasions can even remember when I had the dream. It's a definite memory of the dream, not like some sort of vision. In some instances, I've known not only that I had a dream of the events, but also what was coming next. On a couple of occasions I recall freaking out the people I was with because I knew (and vocalized) what was happening (and being said) next.

What to Do ...

There are actually multiple problems with precognitive dreams and their value or usefulness.

You have to remember the dream. If there is partial recall of the events/information from the dream, you may disregard it or simply not have any information of any use. As detailed elsewhere in this book, just about anybody can learn to remember their dreams, even in the rich detail you might need for utilizing information you peg as psychic.

Even if you remember the dream in full detail, *you must consider the form of the information and whether there's even enough to use.* Psychic information is notoriously partial in nature. As with the dream of the airline disaster mentioned earlier, partial and incomplete information may be basically useless.

If you know a family member will be in a car accident, but the car you see isn't that person's car, which he or she drives every day along the same route you see in your dream, and there is very little other detail (other than, say, that the accident occurs with a blue van), all you can really say to that person is "be wary of blue vans." Remember, though, that you don't want to breed paranoia—such a warning taken too seriously can cause that person to effectively panic at the first sign of a blue van, which in turn could actually cause the accident that you foresaw.

Along with this is the idea that the *information may occur in very symbolic form.* Without being aware that seeing a giant blue beetle chewing on your car is symbolic of a car accident between your car and a blue Volkswagen bug or beetle, means there's no way to interpret and apply that dream information. That also could merely be a dream brought on by watching one too many Japanese monster movies, bearing no symbolic connection to any future event at all.

Another basic problem of utilizing precognitive information is the actual recognition by the dreamer that the dream is important, that it says something about the present or future. You can have lots of dreams that seem to come true after the fact, and those may or may not have been precognitive, depending on how much you read into the symbols of those dreams, and how often you have dreams that don't come true.

If you learn to remember most of your dreams, you really must look at the importance you place on that dream. Most people say that their psychic experiences generally *feel different* than other experiences. It would almost be as though there is some flashing light or asterisk attached to that experience or dream that says "Hey, listen up … this is psychic stuff here … pay attention!" The dream must be recognized and weighed with some sense of it being important before you'd even pay enough attention to it to consider it psychic.

Then, after viewing it as important, there's the issue of acceptance. You have to accept not only that it is potentially psychic and telling you something, but that what it says may not be complete or may be symbolic of something. You'd then have to either consciously analyze what the information might pertain to or go with a gut feeling or sensation that what you can get out of it relates to a particular situation or event or individual.

Furthermore, if you plan to do something with the information, you have to decide just how to apply it. Should you tell the person it might affect (if it affects someone other than yourself)? Will assuming the information is future stuff and accepting it as such make that person (or you) paranoid about that predicted event? Could having knowledge of that event actually cause it to happen? And of course, there is the issue of whether that other person you told would accept the precognitive experience you had or would see you as crazy or having a wild imagination or cause him or her to avoid you like you had "some sort of plague."

Can We Use the Information?

Finally, there is the question I've brought up many times before: Now that you have the information, can anything be done with it?

When we're talking about precognitive experiences, in dreams or in conscious experience, we're back to the idea and problem of just what the future is. If you have a view of a predetermined future, what good is the information? The answer may simply be that such information can psychologically prepare you for the inevitable. I think most of us would be uncomfortable with that. I and many others I know are more comfortable with some sense of empowerment in our lives—that we have some say in the way our futures shape up, some free will in choosing our destiny.

Many psychics and fortune-tellers do not put enough (or even any) emphasis on the control and responsibility we have for our own lives and choices. One of the marks of a good, ethical, psychic practitioner is a proviso with any prediction that the future is ultimately yours to make. Psychic information seems to best be utilized if you see it as pointing to probabilities, to events likely to happen, where you as a participant have some power to cause the event to happen or not happen.

In the past, studies of precognitive experiences that were reported to places like the Central Premonitions Registry, which was run for years in New York City yielded interesting results. The majority of reported precognitive experiences (including dreams) were of events that could have alternate outcomes depending on human intervention. While it would be impossible to stop an earthquake from happening, if your dream provided when and where and how strong it was to be, that information (if accurate and taken seriously) could save lives once people were warned to get out of the area. [Note: there are several websites with some form of "premonitions registry" on the Internet. Just search for the phrase.]

In other words, even seemingly inevitable or unstoppable events and circumstances (such as natural disasters) can have different outcomes depending on whether the precognitive information relating to the people to be affected by the disaster took heed of your warning.

Once again, I must impress upon you that taking the information too seriously can have drastic negative effects as well. Just as a psychic telling you something like "You are about to find a sum of money" might cause you to scan the environment until you find that dollar lying on the sidewalk or all that change in your sofa, a warning of danger could have you checking out your surroundings so cautiously that you actually panic at the first sign of anything resembling that dream, placing you *into* the danger you had hoped to avoid ... a self-fulfilling prophecy.

Then there's the role of coincidence in all of these experiences.

Common Experiences

People *do* have common experiences and yes, fact can be stranger than fiction. I've lived out experiences I have seen also occur in television shows in some similar form (though I'm still waiting to captain a starship). Just because I suddenly recognize a situation I'm in as being just like the one I saw on *Cheers, The Big Bang Theory,* or one of the TV soap operas, doesn't mean I should suspect that the writers of those shows have somehow tuned in to my future (or past or present, for that matter).

Fiction is generally based on, at least partially, real, human experience. While the movie and television show *Alien Nation* was not fact-based (in that there is not a colony of more than 200,000 extraterrestrials living in Los Angeles), it *was* based on people's real experiences of prejudice, bigotry, racism, sexism, religion, and the integration of outsiders into another culture. *Avatar* had significant parallels to what happened to Native Americans. Many episodes of the various *Star Trek* series provided parallels to situations such as those in the Middle East, Northern Ireland, returning veterans, and drug abuse.

Dreams are often similar reflections of common human experience. Coincidentally, a dream you have may relate to a real experience. Events *do* occur by coincidence. This is to be expected.

Skeptics point out that to place value on the precognitive content of a person's dreams, you have to take into account the number of dreams that don't come true or that occur mainly by coincidence. You may be able to judge that a given dream was not likely a precognitive one as it stands alone among all those other dreams that didn't come true, making it statistically insignificant. It also could simply be a coincidence that you dreamed the situation in advance.

If you are looking back after the event, realizing that you had a dream about the event before it happened, whether that was a precognitive dream really can't be determined unless there was a lot of detail recorded before the event, and that detail was specific enough to that event to say it was unique. Of course, to you, the dream may feel different, and that may be what makes it different from something considered purely coincidence.

Use the Info!

So, what if you have the dream and realize before the event that this is about the future? Well, if the other problems, from partial information to recognition of importance to acceptance of the information, are overcome, and you can make use of the information, it doesn't matter if we're speaking of a true knowledge of a future event or simply the mind making an educated guess based on what you already know that something is likely to happen soon. *Use the information.*

For some reason, there seems to be this perception that psychic information may be more knowing of the future than any sort of conscious, rational, logical prediction based on hard information. The answer to this dilemma is perhaps dependent on whether there is a *knowable future* (or even a *probable future* for us to pick up on) and if so, whether it is truly possible for information to come from that future to our present.

Without more knowledge of the workings of time itself, it's probably a question best left for sometime in the future. From a practical perspective, it doesn't matter. If the information is *useful*, whether based in a psychic knowing of the future or on logical, intuitive, emotional, or illogical guesswork, then use it. Take responsibility for creating your own future, and the possibilities may become clearer to you, psychic or not, in your dreams or awake.

Make that future your own.

chapter 11

What Affects Our Psychic Ability: Psi & Psychic Dreams, and Some Theories

Understanding just how psi works and who has more or less psychic ability has been a focus of parapsychologists since the 1960s. It's been determined that we all have some degree of psychic ability, but it is not known what causes a specific psychic experience. Some individuals appear to be more psychic than others, and there are likely influences of both nature and nurture.

Belief in the possibility of psychic ability seems to be an extremely important factor in whether a person has or recognized psychic experiences. In studies of the Sheep-Goat Effect, the term and methodology coined by parapsychologist and psychologist Dr. Gertrude Schmeidler, there is often a significant difference in the experimental results of participants in psi experiments between those who believe in (at least) the possibility of psychic functioning ("sheep") and those who don't (skeptics, disbelievers, or "goats"). This correlation of scoring on ESP and even PK tasks has been seen in many experimental series, with sheep typically scoring above chance and goats typically at or below chance.

We do know that belief may be tied to a performance issue. One who believes in psi may simply have the tendency to perform in psi experiments, in much the same way an athlete or a musician has a better chance of a successful performance if he or she has confidence in his or her performance. Doubt is the performance killer it seems, in a variety of tasks human beings perform. It is also possible that the Sheep-Goat Effect, where it occurs outside the lab linking believers to a higher incidence of psychic experiences, may have more to do with believers (or at least folks who don't discount the existence of psi) being more likely to recognize or categorize an experience as psychic than a disbeliever (or someone simply likely to need to pigeonhole an unusual experience in categories that make sense in terms of what is culturally and/or scientifically accepted today).

Such predisposition toward one thing or away from another, or ideas that shape the way an experience may be perceived, can affect the results people have in a psi task. One may believe in psi but not particularly enjoy a particular kind of experimental task, or may simply not have enough personal confidence in doing well in that task. Think of it this way: this may be similar to an athlete doubting his or her own performance. A pole-vaulter who knows someone can break the record may not have enough confidence to do it himself, even though he's physically capable of it. We all set limits on ourselves in what we can do and how well we can do it. Belief is important in many areas, though we may have a deep-seated sense of what we think we can do, and what things we can excel (or fail) at.

Everyone has psi, but the frequency and strength of psi experiences vary quite a bit, and they appear to depend on many factors beyond belief and preference. It appears that some have a greater degree of control (as much as one can control such an elusive faculty) than others. It may also be that due to our education process, which in our culture seems to ignore or deny such experiences, we may be interacting with the environment constantly on a psychic level and simply not recognizing it. Just as dependency on vision and hearing may cause us to not notice other sensory input as much as we could, our learning to depend on our senses and deny other unusual signals may cause our attention to stray away from psychically derived input and output, except, apparently, where there is a need for us to notice, or a goal to be reached through focused attention on psi.

Remember, having psi experiences is a normal thing. If everyone has these abilities, as studies seem to imply, and if we get reported experiences from people of all ages, nationalities, cultures, religions, and physical conditions, then to have a psychic experience is to be within that range of human behavior we call normal. Not crazy or weird or bizarre, merely normal, if rare for many people. People who reported lucid dreams used to get similar reactions. Of course, with appropriate evidence and presentation, that has changed for lucid dreaming. Hopefully the acceptance of psychic experiences will change someday soon as well.

Effects of Family Belief and Upbringing

In too many families in Western culture, children are told that they "can't know something is about to happen" or "can't make something move without touching it" or "can't know what Uncle Harry is thinking." One certainly *can't* see a real ghost. Such denial of experience, whether it is because a parent thinks the claims are the result of fantasy or whether the negatives come because the parent doesn't believe in the possibility of such things, cause a person to grow up ignoring psychic interactions (since they really *can't* happen), or even to develop a completely closed mind to such things. In either case, both imagination and psi should be fostered and nurtured. We so often tend to set mental limits on what we can do that any process that helps us deny the limits helps us go past them.

In a family with a history of psychic experience, there is naturally going to be an open-minded attitude toward psi. It is therefore difficult to pin down whether a higher number of experiences or a greater control of such abilities is related to heredity or to instilling the abilities into someone (rather than out of them) or a bit of both. It does appear that the abilities do run in a family, pointing at a genetic component. However, this could simply be due to a higher degree of acceptance and therefore recognition of psychic experience in a particular family.

What's the Channel?

The impressions one receives through whatever the psychic channel is are often unreasonable or illogical. A hunch to do something unusual (which later benefits you) is often not in keeping with what one logically sees about a situation. A person who is of an extremely logical nature, who analyzes situations without allowing for solutions from out of left field, may ignore any unusual input (psychic or simply from the subconscious). On the other hand, in looking over the variety of spontaneous cases of psi, it has been seen that there is often an emotional content to well-perceived information. In any case, *thinking* about what may be psychic information, which is so often unreasonable or incomplete, causes that old problem of trying to fit the information into what we already know, while that information may simply not fit.

Creativity

This may be why people of a more creative or artistic nature are seen as more psychic than noncreative people. Dr. Thelma Moss did a study in the late sixties looking at psi abilities of artists versus nonartistic folks. Of course, given what I said above, you can guess that there was a significant difference between the two groups, and that the artists scored above chance. A follow-up poll a couple of years later by another researcher showed a higher percentage of believers among artists than among nonartists. Other studies since then have also indicated that creativity and psi are linked, that creative people are better able to let the psychic information or interaction simply happen, without trying to fit it into one's picture of the way things must work.

Personality

The human personality also has its effects on psychic functioning. For example, extroversion has been tested quite a bit in relation to psi. There is an overall tendency for extroverts (outgoing people) to score above chance. Introverts, who may close themselves off, have the opposite tendency, with chance or below chance scoring more likely. So it appears that there is a better chance for a person to be psychic if he or she is outgoing, creative, and a believer in psi in both general situations and experimental conditions. If that person also grew up in a culture or a family environment where belief in psi was in the open and not denied, there is even a greater chance of psi being evident in his or her life.

These variables, extroversion, belief, creativity, attitude, education, and also mood (the mood one is in while doing the psi task) may influence the entire range of psi. In dealing with emotional states, or moods, there doesn't seem to be any one kind of mood that's best for everyone. Some people have psychic experiences while in what might be considered negative moods (sad, depressed, bored, etc.) while others may be more psychic when they are upbeat (happy, energetic, etc.), but the main functioning of psi points to some kind of goal-directed process.

What It All Means

What we know about psychic functioning indicates a few things. First of all, psi seems to be tied to a variety of psychological factors, from personality variables to emotional moods to belief factors. As a phenomenon so directly related to psychological variables, which are themselves inconsistent, it's no wonder that there is a difficulty in getting an individual to be psychic on demand. We (human beings in general) tend to set our own limitations where psi functioning is concerned. Our culture sets up belief system boundaries around the occurrence and even possibility of psi (remember that science and scientific thought are part of a culture's belief system).

We educate our children out of being psychic. We actually learn, within a cultural context, how to perceive the world around us. As infants and children in a learning context, we are taught to recognize certain shapes, colors, processes, sounds, smells, tastes, textures, and other physical factors. We are told that there are physical laws, and that objects and events behave in certain ways and don't behave in others. That shapes our own perceptions and sets up certain expectations of how things around us should be and how they should behave. This fact, this perceptual expectancy, is a principle magicians make use of all the time with sleight-of-hand effects and illusions.

Other internal factors affect our recognition of and reaction to psychic experience. We each develop some form of internal logic that lets us, as individuals, make sense of the world around us and the behavior of others. We react to observations and experiences by thinking through, categorizing, and cataloging the experience as our logic dictates. We are also feeling creatures, and our emotional reactions to experiences can either help us recognize and react to psychic experience or cause us to ignore or even fear them.

So, while psychic ability is distributed throughout the entire population, some people are likely to be more psychic than others due to the various factors that are related to psi's appearance. It's a normal process (since everyone has it), yet conscious psychic experiences, while not as uncommon as many think, are certainly not as frequent as other kinds of normal experiences—at least for most people.

Yet psi is likely to be happening all the time, just as our other senses are operating at some level almost all the time (although there is no real visual input if you close your eyes), and what we consciously perceive is not always everything we think we receive through our senses. Psychologists have spoken of a cocktail party effect in conjunction with the sense of hearing. Everyone seems to experience this at some time, whether at a cocktail party or not: a crowded room, lots of people talking, and you can change your attention to focus on this person talking, then switch to another, even though it's *all* going into your head.

Think of psi the same way, always operating, but needful of your center of attention. Unfortunately, since we are taught so well by people and our physical environment to use just our normal senses, it may take something with a bit of an emotional punch to become part of your conscious attention, whether that intense signal tells you to stay away from a certain intersection to avoid an accident or it simply gives you the feeling that something happened to Uncle Harry. If that signal can't get your attention with just the bit of information, maybe your subconscious gives it more of a punch by letting you psychically see Uncle Harry.

Always Scanning

What appears to be happening is that your psychic abilities, tied so well into your unconscious thought processes, are scanning the environment, looking for information that is useful or interesting and often something that will divert your attention from what's coming in through regular sensory-perceptual channels. That psi signal may fulfill an emotional, intellectual, or physical need or goal. The whole process may be unconscious, as some part of you, ever vigilant to find information important to your existence or state of mind, continuously scans the environment. The experience of receiving and recognizing that information may happen when there is a bit of information received that meets a need you have (aware of the need or not) or can direct you toward some goal or other. You may be consciously aware of the information piece or not, as you can be unconsciously directed to initiating a particular course of action (such as getting out of the way of a falling piano, even though you never once looked up). Your response may even be an unconscious psychic one, where the reaction is carried out through the use of psychokinetic ability.

Rex Stanford came up with a theoretical construct to cover this idea of scanning the environment, which in parapsychological terms is called a Psi Mediated Instrumental Response (PMIR). You may be aware of all this happening (the entire process, from detection of the need-related info to the action that is taken), or it may all be handled, from start to finish, with unconscious psi processes. A response could be a nagging feeling not to drive your car down a certain street (to avoid a nasty accident) or simply causing a momentary lapse in memory that causes you to go elsewhere (not remembering where you're going) or even a simple mistake you make almost without awareness (like making a wrong turn). In other situations, the PMIR may be psychic in nature, causing you to see an apparition or to have a psychokinetic outburst (as in a poltergeist situation).

There are negatives to this kind of situation as well. While it sounds great that we are constantly scanning for things that will help us out in life, and hopefully responding to fill the needs, there are also opposite possibilities. Not everything we do is positive. If a person holds a negative self-image, it is possible that things will not work out for the better, since a person in that frame of mind may not expect them to. The need that is served may be to perpetuate the conscious image one holds, so one's psi may scan for and lead one into events that would strengthen that image. If the image is negative, the result could conceivably be something like a streak of bad luck. In our dreams, those negative images may appear as nightmares or supposedly evil figures in otherwise sedate dreams. Facing up to such images and asking questions of them serves the purpose of working through any lasting effects of the information that could adversely affect you.

So, it would seem that we are scanning the environment, that we are intimately connected with it in and out of our dreams. That this psychic scanning can also happen while sleeping and dreaming is well-illustrated by the content of so many psychic dreams.

In fact, it is most probable that *because* the normal senses have low input while sleeping that psychic information may be able to come to the dreamer's attention. That, and the acceptance of no rules or laws in the dreamworld, of course.

Let's finish up by talking about how others work with dreams, and how you can, too!

chapter 12
Dreamwork and Dreamweavers

Though the bulk of what I will be covering in the first part of this chapter has to do with nonpsychic dreams, it's important to consider that, in terms of dreamwork, the nonpsychic dream and the psychic dream really differ very little. The major difference is the content, rather than the mode of dreaming. Both kinds of dreams have information in them. A normal nonpsychic dream has information content from our memory and sensory experience. A psychic or paranormal dream has information from those same sources, yet also draws on psi processes to supply information. Making use of, analyzing, or working with our dreams can be very much the same, whether the dream is psychic or not. It's the identification of the information as psychic and therefore applicable in other ways that makes the psychic dream one that has added value (such as application of the information in business, criminal investigation, daily relationships with others, connections to the environment and to other people, or foreknowledge of some impending event, good or bad).

As you've figured out by now, there are a number of reasons to want to work with your own dreams. From a therapeutic perspective, dreams help us understand ourselves and identify our unfinished emotional business and their sources in our own lives. Working with them can provide access to thinking how we might get past such issues. They can allow our problems, and solutions, to play out in symbols and metaphors and stories. And they can allow us to access our true creativity.

Dream Interpretation

For just about anyone willing to look in a book, dream interpretation has been a seemingly simple matter of recalling any images from a dream and looking up such symbols in a volume of dream symbols and meanings. The book would tell you, often with an air of authority, just what that artichoke you ate in your dream meant. Of course, if you check the same symbol in five or six such books, you might easily get five or six completely different meanings for the symbol.

Looking at the many kinds of therapeutic approaches to dreamwork would take a full book in itself, but there are popular and well-known approaches. Freudian psychologists use one way, having to do with Freud's own views of the purpose of dreams, while Jungian therapists work with Jung's concepts of dreams and their functions. Therapists from other schools of psychological thought use the models appropriate to their own approaches to therapy in general. To learn more about specific psychotherapeutic approaches to the place of dreams in therapy and psychoanalysis, I suggest you read more in such areas or contact a therapist who specializes in Jungian, Freudian, Gestalt, or other forms of therapy. Ultimately, it would appear that to really deal with a dream, the interpreter, the therapist, the diviner needs to be *you, the dreamer.*

Be Your Own Interpreter

To quote Dr. Loma Flowers of the Delaney & Flowers Professional Dream and Consultation Center in San Francisco:

> All methods of dream analysis rely on the assumption that dreams have meaning of psychological relevance to the dreamer, but differ in the way that meaning is extracted. The traditional methods of dream interpretation evolved in the context of psychoanalysis and are consequently directed toward analysis of the transference, of the psychodynamic origins of the neurotic conflicts, and toward the collective unconscious. The contemporary eclectic methods are evolving in the context of individual growth—with or without therapy—and are directed more toward insight which can be more immediately applied to daily living. These differences produce variations in interpretation of the same dream. As in psychiatric treatment in general, the goal one is seeking from dream interpretation influences one's approach to the problem and choice of technique. It is therefore important to step back and choose a technique of dream interpretation in light of the results one is seeking and appropriate to the style of therapy being used.
>
> —from "The Morning After: A Pragmatist's Approach to Dreams," by Loma K. Flowers, MD, *Psychiatric Journal of the University of Ottawa,* vol. 2 (1988): 70

Dr. Montague Ullman, a psychiatrist and parapsychologist and coauthor of *Dream Telepathy,* has been a pioneer of the idea that working with dreams does not have to take place only in therapy, that one doesn't necessarily even need a trained therapist in working with dreams. Ullman and others advocate placing dreams in a social context, in sharing dreams with others in a group format so as to really deal with the dreams, rather than to place dreams in a larger context of counseling or therapy.

In formal therapy, which is typically a one-to-one (patient and therapist) relationship or on occasion in group format, there are certain controls the patient gives up to the therapist. The therapist, as the expert consulted by the patient, is in control of any number of things, from the direction the therapist may want to pursue in exploring the patient's psychological makeup to the suggestion of how long therapy may take until it's over and the work is done. This is not to say that a therapist may not ask the patient "What do you want to work on today?" Therapists do that, of course, but always from a place of control of the session and the therapy in general. The roles of therapist and patient are unequal.

Unless the therapy sessions are specifically designed to work with the patient's dreams as source material, rather than all the waking experiences of the patient's past, a dream and its meaning can be lost in the greater context of the overall therapy. If you are in therapy to deal with emotional problems caused by relationships with the opposite sex, the therapist will generally be pulling from the entire scope of your past and present to consider any number of influences on relationships you've had. A dream in such a context becomes simply another source of clues, rather than a means to reveal the problem and deal with it. The dream is only a small part of the work being done by patient and therapist.

In group dreamwork, such as Ullman's format, the dreams of the group members are the central focus of the work to be done by the individuals. The individual dreamers in the group are in control of what they say and how much they reveal to the group. Even the group leader, who acts more as a facilitator of the process rather than as the expert in the group, has an equal role with all others with respect to dealing with the dreams themselves. There is respect by the group members for individual privacy of the group members, for the ultimate authority the individual has over his or her own dreams, and for the uniqueness of the individual that each dream addresses. This does not mean that the group should not be led by a therapist, just that a therapist is not a necessity.

Why Work with Your Dreams?

I asked Pat Kampmeier, a therapist in Marin County, California, about why people should work with their dreams. Pat is a therapist who has done dreamwork for a number of years, in both individual therapy settings and group settings, and is also a student of parapsychology.

> I always tell people that the experience of the dream itself is worth something, even if you do no work with it at all. It opens up a dimension in yourself that helps you feel full and complete. It has characters and feelings and happenings that are not necessarily like your daily life. It's enrichment. Just experiencing the dream, being willing to lie in bed and go over the feelings and feel them deeply, to really just be there with it, changes us.
> —From an interview with Pat Kampmeier, 1990

Remembering...

Before getting directly to psychic dreams, let's examine more closely some fundamentals of working with dreams.

One of the most important points to keep in mind is that to work with dreams you have to *remember* your dreams. While it may work in some situations to rely on spontaneous flashes of what you recently dreamed, to really get into dreamwork, keeping a running record such as a journal of your dreams, is extremely important, according to most of the dreamwork experts out there.

First of all, you need to learn to recall your dreams after you wake up more frequently, more easily, and hopefully in greater detail. People can learn to recall their dreams on a regular, even daily, basis. Techniques used by dream researchers and therapists, and subsequent surveys and studies, indicate that just about anyone can learn and practice some degree of dream recall. Some people are naturally good at recalling their dreams, while others can barely remember getting out of bed to check on the kids during the night, let alone any dream imagery.

There may be some degree of difference in the activity of the brain of those who can and can't recall dreams, although such brain activity may change as an individual becomes one who can regularly recall his or her dreams. Dr. Roseanne Armitage and Tom Fitch at Carleton University in Ottowa, Canada, conducted a study of such differences between those who have a high degree of dream recall and those who have low recall. With the low dream recallers, there appears to be a large shift in electrical activity between the two hemispheres of the brain when awakened from REM sleep, as though the hemispheres are knocked off balance. For those people, sleep and wakefulness are two very different states. For the high recallers, there is very little electrical disruption between the hemispheres when awakened, with what appears to be a greater continuity in brain processes as the sleep transitions from sleep to waking consciousness.

How do you learn to remember your dreams? As with lucid dreaming, psychic experience, or other forms of psychologically related experiences, intention and motivation seem to play a large role. In fact, just the act of getting *interested* in working with your own dreams may have an effect. On starting the research for this book, I began spontaneously recalling more dreams than any other time in my life (except during college when I seemed to be having a number of spontaneous lucid dreams). If you tell yourself over and over, especially before falling asleep, that you *will* remember your dreams and that you *want* to remember your dreams, you have a much better chance of that happening.

To fix the intention in your head, it is important that you provide yourself with something to record the dreams you recall. Most people tend to keep a written journal of their dreams, and they have a notebook and pen or pencil by their bed. On the other hand, some people like to go the electronic route, keeping a voice recorder handy (and these days, there are apps for that!), as it's easier for them to speak into the recorder rather than expending the energy of writing something down on awakening. It might be best to have both forms of recording (writing implements and smartphone or other recorder) simply because you will then have the option of one or the other (or both) on awakening with some dream imagery in your mind. You might also keep a flashlight or small, not-so-bright lamp handy in case you wake up during the dark of the night after a dream.

If you do go the recorder route, I would suggest going back over the recording when fully awake and transcribing the information, adding any additional imagery that may be recalled while doing that. Having a written form of all dream images and other related information allows people to scan quickly for patterns and relationships between dream content and what's happening in their waking lives.

Remember that to really look at your dreams and their place in your life, you also need to be recording information from your awake and conscious states. You probably should choose another time during the day or evening to record such information, so as not to be confusing it with your dream content. Such information will tend to help understand potential sources of the dream imagery. So record the happenings of the day that may relate to any dreams you might have, the events, issues, and emotions that may stay with you. Keep note of that day residue. You might also note any recent events in the news that were of particular interest or upset you, as societal issues on our minds may also play out in our dreams.

Some dreamworkers suggest taking notes during the day if any other dream images are spontaneously remembered, and to keep track of the things during the day that may fall into your dreams later.

The journal process is, as you can tell, something that may require a commitment of a little time and mental and physical energy. However, if you truly wish to work with your dreams, such a commitment is necessary. It is not imperative that you can recall even one dream a night, as many will tell you that even a dream a week, recorded appropriately with day residue and other information, will be beneficial to work with. However, as just about all who work with dreams report, the process of keeping that journal will tend to increase your dream recall, as you recall more and more, your motivation and interest and intention will increase, thereby reinforcing the whole process.

Intention's the Thing

You record the day's events and feelings, you have your journal-keeping devices by your bed, and you're ready to go to sleep. Again, it seems extremely important, at least at the beginning of the practice, to have the intention in mind that you *will* remember your dreams. I've spoken with a number of people who work with their own dreams who repeat that intention mentally every once and a while during all waking hours, to further program themselves for dream recall, though the intention at bedtime alone seems to work.

Upon Waking Up

There are a few points of awakening that might arise within a regimen of keeping the dream journal. Upon awakening just after a dream (or as a result of one), stay relaxed and allow your thoughts to collect themselves and the images to arise. As you have just been through REM sleep, there is a better chance you'll remember the whole dream rather than just fragments of it. You may ask yourself "What was I dreaming?" as suggested by Stephen LaBerge, and allow the images to come forth. It may take only a second or two or a few minutes, and you may recollect the whole dream or just parts of it. As the dream takes form or fragments of the dream come up, focus on them for a moment. Do not try to analyze, identify, or categorize the images, rather just take note of them and allow them to bring out other pieces.

Record the recollections, from the fragmentary or whole dream images to feelings, colors, or anything else that may come to you. You might want to try drawing anything you can, in addition to jotting down or recording the words. When you fall back to sleep, repeat the intent to remember more dreams that night (keep in mind we go in and out of REM sleep a few times during the night).

You may awaken naturally in the morning, though not necessarily after a REM stage, with some dream content floating around in your head. Again, relax and let your mind wander. Keeping your eyes closed appears to help in this process. Even if you don't recollect a dream at all the moment you wake up, the process of asking yourself about your dreams and allowing any images to collect may help recall. Record any images or feelings you get. If you plan on going back to sleep, repeat the recall intention.

Finally, you may awaken because of an alarm of some kind, whether for work or something specific to do during the morning. If you get caught in the middle of REM sleep with that alarm, you could be set to record some rich detail about your dreams. Relax, recollect the images, and record them. If you recall nothing, relax a moment and let your mind wander, and ask yourself what you could have been dreaming. Record whatever you get. Gackenbach and Bosveld (*Control Your Dreams*) suggest that you might set your alarm for a different time, perhaps a half hour earlier, if you don't recall any dreams, since those thirty minutes may place you in a REM sleep stage.

Important for Journal Keeping

It is important to remember a couple of things about the journal process. Record *all* dreams, *all* fragments of dreams, and any other feelings or images that may come to you as a result of the recall process. You must be committed to recording everything and every dream if you want to really work with them.

You should record all images, however, fragmentary. The imperfect memory we seem to have of our own dreams parallels the incomplete information transfer that often accompanies psychic experiences. You might recall an important shape or feeling or color from a dream that can still be related to your waking life without identifying or categorizing that information. In other words, without labeling it "the Eiffel Tower" as opposed to simply recording a dream of a tall, steel lattice shape that might be part of the power station down the street.

With experiments in ESP such as those with remote viewing or the ganzfeld work, parapsychologists have learned that analyzing, categorizing, labeling, or identifying the imagery or other information received often causes our minds to fill in blanks of the actual psychic information with other images that are unrelated to the actual target. In remembering dreams, we might get an incomplete image that we flesh out to fit the label we too quickly put on it. This effectively misidentifies what the dream was about simply because we tend to be frustrated by incomplete pictures. However fragmentary the images are, they typically can relate to a waking event or issue—or psychic perception—regardless of whether they've been identified as "such and such" a person or object or not.

Don't worry about keeping items remembered in any sort of correct time sequence. The order of occurrence of events and images in a dream may be difficult to get straight while conscious, unless of course the whole dream is remembered. With regard to time, it is important to jot down the date and time of the dream or recall, as well as such time information for any waking events recorded, so as to best make use of the journal later.

Regardless of the method of initial recording of the recalled information, whether in written or recorded form, the act of copying or transcribing it into a more permanent notebook or onto a computer tends to bring up more imagery and scenes from the dreams, as well as memories of items needful of recording from waking, conscious time. If you've done any drawings, keep those with the permanent dream journal. Some dreamworkers suggest titling the dreams, as you would a short story.

A review process of the journal is also helpful in reinforcing dream recall. As you go back over previously recorded dreams, you may have new imagery show up or a new feeling arise. Record this information as well, as it is often enlightening in the process of interpreting your dreams and reinforces the motivation and intention of the whole procedure.

Be Your Own Interpreter

In terms of interpretation, remember that you are the best interpreter of your own dreams. The issue of how you work with your dreams is one you may want to look at. As you've read, there are more than a few ways to work with or interpret dreams, whether by yourself, in a one-to-one setting with a therapist or friend, or in a group setting. There are some advantages to each type of setting, as well as differing views on which is more successful.

Ullman and others have advocated bringing dreamwork to the people, so to speak. Working with a therapist may be necessary for some people who need to look deeper into themselves than what their dreams may tell them, and I've already discussed the issue of control in dreamwork settings with a therapist. The one-to-one situation may work well for you if you simply work with a friend or relative who also is working with his or her own dreams, more or less working as a mini dream group. Bouncing the dreams off someone you already trust may alleviate some of the concerns many people have around sharing their innermost secrets with a group of people you must learn to trust. Gayle Delaney suggests telling the dream to the therapist (or other individual or group) as though the listener is an extraterrestrial, perhaps a Martian who knows absolutely nothing about our world, not even what a piece of paper or a banana is or who Elvis Presley or Prince was. This allows for rich detail without labeling.

If you are working with the journal on your own, you should consider Delaney's advice. If I had to describe images from the perspective of including a lot of information that could allow for someone totally unfamiliar with the thing in my image, I could easily avoid identifying that image which in turn would allow for more open (and perhaps easier) connections to my waking life. The Eiffel Tower may mean nothing to me, but the general shape and construction of such a dream image may reveal my unvoiced concern about that electric power structure near my home.

Dream Groups

The group setting is one that does seem to work well for many people because of the commitment involved (in both recording the dreams and participating in the group process) and in the very format that allows the dreamer to stay in control. Ullman's group process involves four stages of discussion of the dream, which I'd like to summarize and comment on.

In Stage I of the group process, the dreamer volunteers a dream, allowing the group to ask questions for clarification so as to grasp the content of the dream as clearly as possible. There is no absolute expectancy that each member of the group has to have had a very recent dream to share, so there is a safety net for those who may not wish to share a dream at a particular session. In addition, the act of relating the dream to a group (or even to an individual) often allows for insight, especially if others ask questions for clarification.

In Stage II, the dreamer sits back and listens as the group discusses the dream and any imagery or feelings or ideas it conjures up for them. The group takes the dream as their own for a time, allowing for free association that may spur on other members of the group with ideas or jog the dreamer's own insight and memory of other dreams or real events. Intuition may play a big role as the group members state their own perceptions and discuss the metaphors that the image may bring to them. The dreamer, now simply an observer, may feel safe in that position as a non-participant, able to accept, deny, or ignore anything heard without offending or affecting anyone else in the group. At the same time, the dreamer is working on his or her perceptions of the dream that have now evolved as part of the group's discussion of the dream.

Stage III returns the game to the dreamer, who responds to the group discussion with how his/her understanding and perception of the dream has been affected, evolved, changed, or grown. The control of the dream and discussion of it is back with the dreamer, who may elicit further discussion and dialogue directly from the group. The group may prompt the dreamer with further questions for clarification or suggestions of connections, but it is the dreamer who may share, hold back, or accept whatever it is from his/her waking life that can now be related to the dream. The dreamer has the right of control, the right to respond, ignore, accept, deny, or ask for further comments and questions from the group.

Stage IV involves a review of the dream by the dreamer alone sometime between that group meeting and the next. During that interval, the dreamer should revisit the dream in light of everything that came out during the last group meeting and discussion of the dream, noting any further ideas or interpretation of the dream. This allows the dreamer a greater freedom of working with the dream with a richer, more detailed information base to draw on (the dream's content plus whatever came up during the working of the dream by and with the group).

The group process does require a commitment and an investment of regular time, as any process of therapy may involve (although if you look at a therapistless dream group as therapy, it is self-controlled therapy).

On Your Own

If you want to work alone, you are among many others of similar intent. While any dreamwork does require commitment and some amount of time, working alone does so without the rigid schedule a group or one-to-one format may require. Once you have that dream journal going, and you are recalling and recording dream imagery on a regular basis, you can begin to review the journal for patterns and suggestions of connections and relationships to your conscious life. Let me reiterate that it is important to not only record the dreams (or dream fragments) themselves, but also whatever strikes you from your waking day. Also, as you copy over your brief notes to a more permanent journal or computer record, jot down any associations you may get from the dream characters, objects, or events.

Ask yourself questions as you review your dreams, such as "Now why did I dream that?" in order to bring up associations to waking life, and jot them down. Gayle Delaney, in her book *Living Your Dreams,* suggests that we look at dreams as we would a theatrical or film production, where you are the producer, director, writer, special effects person, and actor(s). You might ask yourself questions like "Why did I write this scene this way? Why did I write it at all?" or "Why did I direct the characters to act this way?" or "What's my motivation or emotion for this scene?" or "Where does this scene (dream) fit in to the overall plot of my life?"

In interpreting dreams, whether from a series or singly, you need to remember that dreams are often metaphors for situations or concerns from our waking lives. Look at how the actions, events, characters, and objects may have different meanings for you and try to collect a series of symbolic meanings for yourself. In other words, you might learn from reviewing your dreams that certain things appear more than once in your dreams and represent specific things to you each time they appear.

Our dreams typically concern us directly, with the exception of some psychic dreams that may reach beyond an immediate impact on us. Often the imagery in our dreams does concern situations of immediate concern (same day) and can be easily read from the dream. Other imagery may reappear in dreams because it points to a continuing concern or problem or interest. What's important is to remember that the dreams have their place in your own life and should be looked at as both literal representations as well as symbolic ones.

Easy Answers?

Dream experts say that the methods of both dream recall and interpretation are fairly easy to learn, and they appear to work for just about anyone. On the other hand, the commitment to keeping a journal (very regularly) and the continual time expenditure in the recall, recording, and reviewing process is difficult for some people. You, the dreamer, need to decide if you really want to do it; if you're motivated to do it. Remember that such intent and motivation seem to be a necessity to any dream recall or interpretation process.

You may be able to program yourself to remember your dreams, and also to wake up each time you have a dream, which should in turn increase recall. Some people are able to do this with a simple addition to the statement of intent (to recall dreams) you go through at bedtime. Repeating to yourself "I will remember my dream as soon as I wake up, and I will wake up as soon as I finish a dream" may push the program along. In any event, the process of programming yourself is not a fast one, and may take many weeks rather than a few days. But it does seem to work for just about anyone, so don't be discouraged. You can do it if you believe you can.

So, what you need to balance against the downside, the commitment of time and energy, is the potential payoff of working with your dreams. Dreams appear to help us learn and may aid in memory formation. They can help us to approach and work through traumatic events in our lives. They can relate to our past history or to very immediate events in our lives. They are providers of what is often the most honest information we offer to ourselves. They can help us understand ourselves more thoroughly, from our fears and anxieties to our hopes and dreams for life (no pun intended). They enlighten us to our own connectedness to others and to the world around us. They can provide us with in-depth information on how we really feel about events in our society. They can be utilized for stress reduction. They may provide creative insights or solutions to problems that are bugging us. They can be means of escape and entertainment.

They are a natural resource for all people.

Dreams for Problem-Solving

Besides the idea of working with dreams to find out more about ourselves, there is the application of using dreams for decision-making and problem-solving. As business and management training is now including some emphasis on intuitive and creative problem-solving, techniques of dreamwork are being included in this instruction. "Sleeping on it" is not a far-fetched method of coming to a decision, and some, notably Gayle Delaney, have written on the incubation of a dream in order to look for solutions to specific problems.

This technique, according to Delaney, is fairly simple but requires commitment, as with other techniques of dreamwork. Keeping the dream journal is an integral part of the incubation of a dream, as review of the journal is essential. You must choose a good time, a good night to work on a specific problem, and it should be one when you are not too tired and have not been drinking alcoholic beverages or taking drugs that could affect your sleep. You want to review your dream journal before going to sleep, taking note of the day's happenings and feelings. You need to have an internal discussion of the problem to be solved, thinking it through from any number of angles so as to decide what needs to be addressed and what kind of information would provide a working answer. Bring up and note any feelings that may be associated with the problem.

Next, you need to come up with an *incubation phrase*, a one line question or request that provides a succinct description of the problem, showing a clear and deep understanding of the situation to be addressed. This should be your final decision of what to incubate, what the dream will address.

Focus on that incubation phrase as you go to bed (and to sleep), leaving that uppermost in your mind—along with the intent to remember the dream. On awakening, go through the recall and recording process, reviewing the information provided by the night's dream(s) for possible solutions to the problems.

Many people have had a good deal of success with using their dreams to solve problems, whether through the purposeful method of dream incubation, or simply through the process of keeping and reviewing the journal. Often the solutions and information provided seem to be from some source outside the experience of the dreamer. While some of that may be intuitive solutions pulled together by the subconscious from seemingly unrelated memories, some of it seems to be from outside ourselves, as though the part of us that was dreaming was truly able to get information from outside sources. That, of course, leads us back to psychic dreams.

chapter 13

Working with Psychic Dreams and Experiences

In working with psychic experiences in general, there is an implicit assumption that we can easily separate a psychic experience from any other experience at the time the experience is happening. While that may be true for some forms of psychic experience, where you immediately somehow know that the experience is different from so-called normal ones, we've learned that dreams can be a bit tricky.

In general, our dreams reflect a connection to our inner selves, even if the dream is of an international-scope event that may not touch us directly. Seeing or hearing about the event in the news can often affect our dreams and reflect our reactions to it. Psychic experiences in general and psychic dreams in particular may be psychic perceptions of what is important to us personally, information sought out by some part of us to incorporate into our lives, or of events that we personally see as important to our views of the world. They may also be psychic perceptions of highly emotional events that have nothing to do with us or what we are interested in.

There appear to be two things happening within our psychic experiences. On the one hand, we seem to be scanning the environment for information that will somehow be of interest to us, to our lives in general or to the solving of some problem we are connected to. On the other hand, we seem to also pick up random signals. An analogy might be to radio scanners, where a radio operator is scanning for a signal from the local police or fire department. The operator might scan until hearing a snatch of conversation that indicates the source is the one desired. There may, however, be another source transmitting very powerfully yet with no particular target in mind (like a call for help from a disabled vehicle or aircraft in trouble). The signal may be strong enough for the scanner to zero in on, even though the intent to pick it up was not in the radio operator's mind.

Our dreams, as random as they appear to be, do have their patterns, which are often discernible by looking through a series of dreams in a journal. With psychic dreams, random signals from the outside appear to drop in, whether we are looking for patterns or not. These random signals, having nothing to do with our own lives (though potentially important to others), may cause a person working with his or her own dreams to pause and puzzle over it, trying to make the item fit in with other imagery in dreams.

So, if you accept the idea of psychic information and that we may occasionally get random signals, you have to allow for some items appearing in your dream journal to be glitches that you may have to leave out of the interpretation process. Such psychic glitches may be later connected to real events in the world, or you may never find out about the event to which the information belonged. Otherwise, much of the information from dreams you know are psychic can be connected to your own life or knowledge base and can therefore be learned from as easily (or as hard) as other dreams.

Looking for psychic information in dreams really is an extension of recalling, recording, and reviewing your dreams using a dream journal. When jotting down imagery and feelings from dreams, if one of those feelings is that you are sure there is something different or psychic about the dream, *make a special note of it.* Over a period of time, you might note specific patterns of emotions, issues, or images in both your waking state and your dreams at the time of the psychic dream.

People who report psychic dreams on some kind of regular basis are usually able to discern the differences between a paranormal and a normal dream in their journals. They have learned through their own experience that the dream is of a particular form, that it may carry something extra. Unfortunately, there is no single method or concept I can now relate to you that would enable you to immediately categorize your dreams as psychic or not. Keeping the journal and reviewing it and your experience with particular dreams will lead you to find your own way of being aware that the dream is something out of the ordinary, perhaps carrying psychic information.

As you work through any dreams you consider psychic, also look at the type of psychic dream it was. Here are some questions you should ask/address:

- Are your psychic dreams mainly precognitive or telepathic?
- Are they perceptions of real-time events or past situations?
- Are they happening during the lucid dream state or when you feel you may be having an OBE-type dream?

- Which type is more frequent?
- Are there particular events, issues, or emotions connected with each type of psychic dream you have?
- Do you feel a character in your dreams was really some contact by another person, living or dead?
- Are you having apparitional encounters in your dreams?

Hopefully, the information I've offered you in this book, along with the various examples of psychic dreams and comments by others has helped you in understanding what you might consider a psychic dream or experience, and what forms it may take.

Pattern Recognition

It all boils down to looking for patterns in your dream experiences. This pattern recognition is also important if you are trying to work on psychic abilities while awake. Keeping a journal of unusual waking experiences, especially ones that might be psychic, and looking for patterns in them seems to allow people to recognize that they have been having psychic experiences of one sort or another all along. However, as with dream journals where you're noting all perceptions remembered from the dreams, working on psychic ability while awake requires some degree of observation of the physical world around you. It is only after you can really, consciously be aware of your normal perceptions (though the normal senses), that you can start to recognize the extra information that may be coming into your head.

Notice You're Already Psychic

So, you might try simply exercising your powers of observation on a regular basis. *Notice* sights, sounds, smells, and other sensations, and notice your own mental and emotional states throughout the day. Look at the relationship of things and people around you to your moods and physical feelings. If you are having psychic experiences, keep track of how you are feeling physically, mentally, and emotionally, before, during, and after the experience. Note what you've eaten, and if there are any unusual situations going on in your life, any concerns, stresses, or other interpersonal reactions. Transfer it all to a journal, as with a dream journal (and you may even want to keep both journals going, to get a full understanding of both waking and sleeping consciousness in your life).

By observing your personal circumstances and feelings while having psychic experiences, you can look for patterns that may lead to or cause the experiences. You may then be able to narrow down what motivates you to be psychic, and devise some exercise to repeat the experiences. The more you learn about when and why you have your experiences, the more you may be able to control their appearance and direct the abilities. If you are not having such experiences, this exercise may not only help your powers of observation, it may also allow you to notice experiences that you had not considered as psychic before. However, don't go overboard in labeling things as paranormal, since you may end up misleading yourself about how truly psychic you are, which can cause some problems.

There's also the flip side here that this exercise is a good way to actually get rid of unwanted psychic experience. By seeing the patterns in your life that may cause the experiences, you can learn what you need to do to avoid them.

Program Psychic Dreams

Do try incubating a dream with the intent to seek out information that may not be within your own experience or memory. Repeat to yourself that there is a target or a location you'd like to dream about and what that target is, incubate a dream for information about a future event or one in the distant past and see what comes up, ask for a solution to a problem even though you have no direct physical access to the information that may provide the solution, or ask for a message or contact from a friend or loved one who has recently died. Remember to try to verify, as best you can, any information that comes through in such dreams, for if you don't relate the information to the real world, you cannot be sure you made the psychic connection.

We are still ignorant about how psychic functioning might work and how to make it work on a more regular, repeatable, reliable basis, both in our conscious waking state or in the dream state. In a few pages, I'll provide some specific experiments you can try to bring about psychic dreaming of varying types.

Dreamwork and Psychic Dreaming

In the process of working with dreams, psychic dreams may appear. Some of these may be problem-solving dreams that include information we could not possibly have known from outside sources. Some may be dreams of events that we don't connect with at the time, later learning that the dream predicted that later event. The dreams may be of events from the past, present, or future, and may be about events or people directly connected to us or far removed from our own lives.

Working with psychic dreams is often the same process as working with any other kind of dream. Psychic dreams are simply those with extra added value—more information from sources outside your sensory experience. One can work with psychic dreams in the same way one works with the nonpsychic variety. The idea of incubating a particular question or problem, even if you don't think you have the answer to it, coupled with a willingness to accept (or even to seek out) information through some psi channel, can yield wonderful psychic results.

But what's important about working with your dreams is not strictly whether it contains psychic information or not, but whether the information *can be used* in a way that is pertinent or applicable to your life.

One difference between the content of the psychic and non-psychic dream is that, for many people, psychic dreams contain information that is not directly applicable to the dreamer. If I dream about a murder or a disaster in some other location (and nowhere near me), that information, if truly psychic, may have no value in my life. However, if that dream of disaster was not psychic, if the information came up from my subconscious, it may be a representation, a metaphor for something *in* my own life.

This leads to the all-pervasive question: How do you know a dream is psychic or not? There are many answers to that question, and many viewpoints. But perhaps the most consistent answer one gets when asking someone who thought a dream he/she had was psychic (which was later confirmed) was that it "felt *different.*"

Dr. Beth Hedva, a psychologist who currently (2016) resides in Canada, was a colleague of mine in the Bay Area during the 1980s. She is someone with extensive personal psychic experience, who is well versed in parapsychological work and dreamwork. I interviewed her for the original version of this book (in

1990), and she had a very succinct response when I asked "How do you know it's a psychic dream?"

> Dreams are multidimensional, and there's a level that I think also includes the transpersonal and spiritual domain. Those dreams in particular contain a quality—it feels almost realer than real—the colors are brighter, the light is a little more refined, the conversations seem more fluent. You're able to remember specifics that in some way allow you to feel as though you've really contacted a person, or seen someone, as though you've been with them. The level of memory is more defined, the textures or smells or qualities.
>
> Somehow when you wake up from a dream like that, there's a feeling that something has happened, something real has happened. It's something more than just a dream, and it doesn't just evaporate during the course of the day. Something remains about that dream, and I think that's a really good signal that there's something more happening for us.

In my discussion with Montague Ullman in 1990, he had this to say about psychic dreams:

> There are people over the years who have written to me and said they have paranormal dreams and that they know when these occur. The only thing I can pick up from these various reports is that they feel these dreams are different from their ordinary dreams and that an image appears in those dreams that they have previously associated with

paranormal and precognitive dreams, or just by the very feeling of urgency to share it or do something about it, the dream is paranormal, but there is no single, consistent one.

With psychic dreams, discussions of the dreams may be the final deciding factor in recognizing the dream as a perception of a real event, past, present, or future.

If you don't tell the person you dreamed about that you had that dream, how will you ever learn if that person shared the dream? If you don't verify, in some way, the information you think came from a real current or past event, how will you ever know if the perception in the dream was correct?

And if you don't either record the dream or discuss it with someone else, how can you be sure you dreamed the event before it actually happened? It might have been faulty memory.

What Can You Do (Next)?

If you can put together a group for working with dreams, that's a wonderful thing, although I don't feel that's the only way. First of all, a group is not always easy to get together. Secondly, it's hard to say just how many people might make a good group. In addition, the methods of controlling your own dreams, whether incubating on a problem or initiating a lucid dream session is pretty much a solitary practice. The dream group (or even one other person with whom you are discussing your dreams on a regular basis) can help you work through the dreams and understand the patterns or specifics they may present, but without you, the dreamer and your own dreams, the group process falls flat.

So, do start out with the intention to work with your own dreams. You can try to notice psychically derived information or even prompt the dreams to go in such directions.

Throughout the book, I've given you pointers to remember and work with your dreams that bear driving home, even if it is repetitive. So, if you decide to work with dreams to initiate psychic experience, you must do a few things first.

Keep a dream journal or log. Get into the habit of recording your dreams on a regular basis. Remember that the *intent* to do this is often necessary to increase dream recall, just as such intent or motivation to be psychic is often necessary to have repeated psychic experiences. Keep note of anything out of the ordinary, how well (or poorly) you slept, how tired you were when you went to bed, what you ate, how you woke up, what your mood was when you went to sleep, any issues on your mind, and how much (or how little) sleep you had. If a dream was particularly striking (or seemed different, lucid, or even psychic) make a special note.

Make the intent to dream and *remember* your dreams become a part of the daily routine. The more you remember and record in your journal, the more you will remember your dreams.

Review the dream journal on a regular basis. Look for patterns in the dreams, both in the content of the dreams as well as how striking or unusual any of the dreams might have been. Look for connections between certain dream images (or how they felt) and the physical factors (how tired, what you ate, how much sleep, etc.) and psychological factors (mood, intent, issues on your mind, etc.). If you begin to see patterns, make special note of them in your journal.

If there are patterns noted, you might try to see if you can repeat the pattern-related dream purposefully. If, for example, you've noticed the same images in dreams popping up (or dreams of flying/out-of-body experiences) when you are in a particular physical or emotional state, you might try re-creating this state to see if the same kind of dream recurs. However, be cautious with this. I don't condone or suggest including the use of any drugs, illegal or otherwise, prescribed or not, in this sort of experiment. In addition, be very careful how you play with your physical and emotional state. If the pattern you're noticing includes a physical state of less than a healthy amount of sleep or not eating properly, you need to consider if the end result (the dream) is worth the price (ill health). I don't believe it is.

If you are already having dreams you consider psychic, whether telepathic, clairvoyant, or precognitive, look carefully at the patterns, not only when the dreams happen (and your physical and emotional states) but also the kinds of psychic information (telepathic, etc.), the people/events being connected to, or the general themes of the experiences (disasters, illness, good happenings, friends, relatives, strangers, famous people, etc.).

If you have a dream you believe is psychic, check it out against existing information. If you have a telepathic dream, check the information with that person. If you have a clairvoyant dream of an event or a location, try to match the information with the reality. If you have a dream of the future, keep an eye on the news to see if it comes true, or, if it is a situation you can reasonably interact with, use the information to help or hinder the predicted outcome.

Caution: Always remember that there *may* be nothing you can do to change the outcome of a predicted event. By this, I don't mean that the future can't be changed, just that we can't always be in a position to change it regardless of how much we know. If I know (from a dream) that a political figure is to be assassinated, there may be nothing I can personally do to change that (unless I had very specific information I could relay to that person's security personnel). *I cannot allow myself to either take responsibility for the event or feel guilty that I couldn't alter the outcome.*

Tell yourself repeatedly (along with "I will remember my dreams") that you will have a psychic dream ("I will have a dream dealing with the big meeting I have next week" or "I will connect telepathically with my friend Chris" or "I will go out of my body in my dreams and visit Moscow"). Incubate an issue for which you may have no information stored in your memory and connect it to being psychic to find the answer.

Psychic Dreaming Experiments from Home

Experiments with dreams can only be conducted after you begin the process of remembering and recording your dreams. Otherwise, you may have a momentary satisfaction that the process to have a psychic experience while dreaming worked, but no real remembrance of what it was about. The following exercises naturally follow after you have begun the recall and recording of your dreams.

Clairvoyance/Remote Viewing: Where the target locations or events are current to the time of the dream.

1. Select a location somewhere in your geographic vicinity where you've never been. Do not go to that location until after the experiment. Incubate/think about visiting this location in your dreams. Record dreams over a period of time (say a week)

and pick out any content you think might be related to that location. Copy that down separately.

Take that copy as well as the journal entries of the experiment week to the target location. Compare the information you identified as being related to the actual physical location. Then look through the journal entries for any other descriptions that may be related.

Consider how well you did, including why you thought some content you picked out as related wasn't and why some descriptions you didn't pick out were related.

Try this with more distant locations (which you may have to find photos or descriptions of or someone who is from there, or who lives there currently to learn if your dreams were accurate).

2. Select an event that will occur somewhere in the world during the time you'll be asleep. Go to bed with the intent that you will observe the event in your dreams. Record the information/content of the dreams upon awakening, then through the media or witnesses who may have been there, compare the content of the dreams to the actual events.

Keep in mind that simply dreaming of the outcome of a sporting event or battle that occurs while you are asleep does not necessarily mean you had a psychic experience. It's also possible that your dreaming mind made a good guess. Look more closely at the descriptive content of the dreams (it's not who wins or loses, but descriptions of how the game was played). Try this on several nights to see what kind of hit rate you get.

3. Arrange with a friend (who is anywhere but at your location) who will be awake and doing something (preferably not

something that could later cause embarrassment) while you are asleep to take note of what s/he is doing during that time period. Record your dream content and compare it with notes taken by your friend. How well did you pick up on your friend's activities?

Telepathy in Your Dreams: The target is a living person and what he or she dreams or has in his or her mind.

1. Have a friend select a number of pictures or illustrations from books or magazines, trying to make them as different from each other as possible. Do not have your friend show them to you.

On specific nights, have your friend select one of these pictures and concentrate on it during the time you are to be asleep. On the same nights, program yourself to dream of what your friend is looking at.

Upon awakening, take down as much information as possible. Then get together with your friend and see how much of your dream, if anything, corresponds with the actual target picture.

2. As a variation of the above experiment, have your friend study the picture before going to sleep. Both you and your friend should record your dreams for that night, then compare them both to the target picture and to each other's dreams. You may find a correspondence to either the picture or to a dream your friend had that had nothing to do with the picture.

3. Make a conscious agreement between yourself and a friend/lover/relative who can also recall his or her dreams (at least to some degree) that you will share a dream. One of you, without telling the other, should then program yourself to dream of a certain topic, event, or issue.

On awakening, both of you should record your dreams and compare notes. Besides the contents of the dream, did you each dream of the other? Did you both show up in the dream?

4. Make a conscious agreement between yourself and a friend/lover/relative who can also recall his or her dreams (at least to some degree) that you will share a dream. Program yourselves, not with an issue to dream, but simply with the idea that whatever the dream(s) you will share it/them.

On awakening, both of you should record your dreams and compare notes. Did you have the same dream? Did you both show up in the dream?

Precognitive Dreams: Here you'll work with targets selected after the dreams are recorded.

1. Program yourself to dream of a friend visiting a location he or she has never been to before (preferably a local one). Spend a week on such programing, recording your dreams each day. Select the content or descriptions you think may relate to your friend.

Have your friend go to a location in your vicinity he or she has never been to (you might have the friend make the selection from a map just before going to the target location). Accompany your friend to the just-selected location and compare your dream notes to the actual location.

2. As a twist on the above experiment, dream of a location you will visit on an upcoming business trip or vacation (again, one which you'd never been to before). Record your dreams up until the time of the visit and compare with the actual location.

3. Have a friend select a fairly large number (say twenty-five) of pictures or illustrations from books or magazines, trying to make them as different from each other as possible. Do not have your friend show them to you.

On specific nights, program yourself to dream of the next day's target. Record the dreams you have that night and have your friend select a target picture from the group. Then get together with your friend and see how much of your dream, if anything, corresponds with the actual target picture.

4. As a variation, your friend could select the pictures and seal them in opaque (preferably very thick) envelopes. After waking up and recording your dreams, select a target from among the envelopes, open it, and compare to your dream journal.

5. Select a topic or an issue that will have some activity in the immediate future or a particular personality to focus on who will be doing something (whatever it is) in the immediate future. This should be something you can either check out in person or through the news media, such as the activity of a celebrity (which has not been announced or decided upon at the time you go to sleep), or where the next earthquake or tornado will occur somewhere in the world, or what event will occur next in the Middle East, or even what will occur in the life of a friend over the course of the next few days.

Focus on the selection and program yourself to dream about it/he/she/them. Record your dreams on awakening, and continue the process over a few days. Each day, you should compare what you've recorded with whatever you can find out about the selected target.

6. As a variation, make your own life the target. Keep track of how your dreams correspond (or don't correspond) to actual events in your life. This will probably work best if you designate specific time periods (say "next Thursday") as the target.

Why These Exercises?

If you begin to find connections between your dreams and outside experiences and events, especially experiences and events for which information you have could not have come through your own sensory experience, memory, or logical inference, you may actually begin having more vivid psychic experiences in your dreams (and likely in your waking life) without having to program for them.

It would appear that for people who accept psychic experience into their lives, who welcome it and are not afraid of it, the more experiences you notice and the more experiences you'll have.

And of course, the more you begin to recall and record your dreams, the more dreams you'll recall and be able to record.

Don't be discouraged if the above exercises don't work right away. For many of us, no matter how much we want to have a psychic experience, it appears that we still have our deep-seated blocks and fears of them, due to the way we were all raised and educated in a society that typically downplays, ignores, disregards, or ridicules such experiences. As you try more and more to have such experiences, as you begin to take note of what is a normal experience, you will begin to notice the extras that peek through, both in your dreams and in waking reality.

Keep on dreaming. Psychic or not, the lessons to be learned through our dreams can help us through our own lives and in connecting with the lives of others and the world around us.

Dreams can pick up on two realities, it seems: the reality that is our own experience, awareness, personality, and subconscious view of the world around us, and the reality that is how we connect to other people and to the world around us, the psychic connection to the reality of the world.

Try these exercises for a while. I predict you will be very surprised with how successful you are.

chapter 14
Dream a Little Dream of Conclusions

Throughout this book, we've talked about dreams, sleep, psychic experience and ability, and the nexus of all of these: *psychic dreams.* Hopefully, I've presented answers to questions you've had in all of these areas as well as raised some questions in your mind. The questions you now have may, in fact, outnumber the answers. That is as it should be.

In my own studies of paranormal experiences and parapsychology, I've learned a great deal from the literature of the field; from experimental reports; from attending parapsychological conferences; by conversing with others in the field, including psychics and mediums to skeptics and critics; and from the few psychic experiences I've been lucky enough to have myself. As someone in the field of parapsychology who has sought out publicity and the use of the mass media in order to provide accurate information about the paranormal to the general public, I have been contacted by hundreds of people each year with some question about psychic experiences, or some report they wish to make about their own experiences. So, most of all, I've learned from the experiences of people like you, the reader of this book.

Parapsychology, as a science still trying to stand on its own two feet, has taken on a group of human experiences that appear to be indications that the human mind/consciousness/soul/spirit is capable of vastly more than what we consider within the range of normal experience. Parapsychology looks at experiences that suggest that the mind has information and communication processes that extend beyond the walls of the human skull and the limitations of the senses, experiences that indicate some form of interaction between the mind and the physical environment around it, and experiences that seem to signify that the consciousness is capable of some separate existence from the brain that spawned it. As I've indicated, there are many questions, both in my field and science in general, that are still necessary to answer (let alone address) before we figure out what these experiences are.

Studies of dreams, psychic and otherwise, indicate that there is an extensive information and/or memory process happening in the brain and mind during a different state of physical being from the conscious one—that being sleep. I've discussed what we apparently know or assume about the workings of the brain with regard to dreaming, as well as various ideas and theories that try to explain how dreaming happens, what effect it has on us, and how it works within our own psychological setup. Of course, given the conflict between some of these concepts, you can easily get the idea that there is much we still need to know about the place of dreams in our lives.

I believe what you should have gotten from this book are two things:

First, I hope that leaving you with the understanding that the process of science, whether physical or social science, is something that never stands still. Hopefully (but not realistically) scientists are people who are in a constant state of learning more in order to better understand the universe around us, and humans specifically. There is much we still need to know about the workings of the human brain before we can make more sense of how the mind works (even what it is) and how the brain/mind combination affects both our physical and psychological makeup. Science is a search for questions that hopefully make sense of the answers provided by the world around us and within us.

A next step in that line of thinking leads me (and hopefully you) to realize that parapsychology, dealing with the human mind (which we know so little about) and certain aspects of physics and biology that we are still learning about, is not at a stage where extensive explanations can be given about subjective paranormal experiences. Parapsychology is studying experiences that need much in the way of expansion of our understanding of the mind/body connection and in the understanding of the physical world before an understanding of them may be complete in any way. After more than 130 years of psychical research (but much less time in studying psi experimentally), what is really clear is that we may not be there yet in approaching an understanding of the workings of psychic experience, just as we're not there yet in fully understanding the human brain and/or mind, or even a consensus in science as to the definition of consciousness. As the knowledge base of science grows and there is more for parapsychologists to draw on, we will undoubtedly come closer to that understanding of what psi is or is not.

The second, and more important, lesson I hope you've learned is that while there is much we do *not* know about dreams and psychic experience, there is much we *do* know about how we can integrate such experiences and mental states into our own lives. Regardless of what psychic experience is (or is not), there is something to be learned from such experience. Whether dreams are a byproduct of neuron firings in the brain (as Hobson theorizes) or are a deliberate means of the brain/mind to process and integrate information, we can learn from them and what they tell us about ourselves. People *are* working with their dreams right now. People *are* able to program themselves to recall and record their dreams. People *are* able to incubate dreams to address particular issues and problems in their lives in order to provide themselves with solutions. People *are* able to "wake up" in their dreams, to become lucid and consciously aware in this seemingly nonconscious state. And people *are* able to use their dreams as a vehicle for connecting with other minds and with the world around them—past, present, and apparently future.

Whether you decide to use the information from this book to look at whatever dreams you might spontaneously remember or whether you decide to pursue the process of working with your dreams, psychic or otherwise, remember that we are all psychic to some degree, which means that some of the myriad dreams will provide information from beyond your own experience and range of normal perceptions. Even if you keep no journal, you might want to ask yourself (at bedtime) to remember your dreams in the morning, and to seek out information and answers that might help you in your daily, waking life. While it's cool (to some) or scary (to others) to think we can get such information psychically, what's most important is that dreams can give us ways to help us understand ourselves and others around us.

Maybe if all the leaders of the world shared the same dream one night ... now *that* would be a great dream.

Through understanding and acceptance of our own experiences we become fuller human beings. As humans we can always learn from our own experiences, no matter how silly or how painful they may be. What we call psychic experiences are no exceptions. Given that dreams are a free avenue for the mind to play at being psychic without the restraints (belief and otherwise), our conscious minds often place on such experiences, dreams are extremely fertile ground for us to *be psychic.*

So tell yourself "it's okay to dream" and "it's okay to be psychic" and that it's certainly "okay to be psychic and dream at the same time."

Dream on and learn...

Bibliography

Auerbach, Loyd. *ESP, Hauntings and Poltergeists: A Parapsychologist's Handbook.* New York: Warner Books, 1986; Martinez, CA: Loyd Auerbach, 2016.

Bro, Harmon. *Edgar Cayce on Dreams.* New York: Warner Books, 1968.

Campbell, Joseph. *The Hero with a Thousand Faces.* Princeton, NJ: Princeton University Press, 1968.

Cartwright, Rosalind. *Night Life: Explorations in Dreaming.* New York: Prentice-Hall, 1980.

Delaney, Gayle. *The Dream Interview: A Refreshingly Practical Approach to Dreaming.* New York: Bantam Books, 1989.

———. *The Hidden Language of the Heart: Unlocking the Secrets of Your Dreams.* New York: Bantam Books, 1989.

———. *Living Your Dreams.* San Francisco: Harper & Row, 1988.

Dunne, J. W. *An Experiment with Time.* London: Papermac, 1981.

———. *The Serial Universe.* London: Faber & Faber, 1934.

Evans, Christopher. *Landscapes of the Night: How and Why We Dream.* New York: Pocket Books, 1983.

Faraday, Ann. *The Dream Game.* New York: Harper Paperbacks, 1990.

———. *Dream Power.* New York: Berkley Books, 1980.

Freud, Sigmund. *The Interpretation of Dreams.* New York: Avon Books, 1966.

Gackenbach, Jayne, ed. *Sleep and Dreams: A Sourcebook.* New York: Garland Publishing, 1986.

Gackenbach, Jayne, and Jane Bosveld. *Control Your Dreams.* New York: Harper & Row, 1989.

Gackenbach, Jayne, and Stephen LaBerge. *Conscious Mind, Sleeping Brain: Perspectives on Lucid Dreaming.* New York: Plenum Press, 1988.

Garfield, Patricia. *Creative Dreaming.* New York: Ballantine Books, 1976.

———. *Your Child's Dreams.* New York: Ballantine Books, 1985.

Green, Celia. *Lucid Dreams.* London: Hamilton, 1968.

Harary, Keith, and Pamela Weintraub. *Have an Out-of-Body Experience in 30 Days: The Free Flight Program.* New York: St. Martin's Press, 1989.

———. *Lucid Dreams in 30 Days: The Creative Sleep Program.* New York: St. Martin's Press, 1989.

Hartmann, Ernest. *The Nightmare: The Psychology and Biology of Terrifying Dreams.* New York: Basic Books, 1984.

Hobson, J. Allen. *The Dreaming Brain.* New York: Basic Books, 1988.

Jung, Carl. G. *Dreams.* Princeton, NJ: Princeton University Press, 1974.

Krippner, Stanley, ed. *Dreamtime & Dreamwork.* Los Angeles: Jeremy P. Tarcher, 1990.

Krippner, Stanley, and Joseph Dillard. *Dreamworking: How to Use Your Dreams for Creative Problem Solving.* Buffalo, New York: Bearly, Ltd., 1988.

LaBerge, Stephen. *Lucid Dreaming.* New York: Ballantine Books, 1985.

LaBerge, Stephen, and Howard Rheingold. *Exploring the World of Lucid Dreaming.* New York: Ballantine Books, 1990.

Lang, Andrew. *Dreams and Ghosts.* Hollywood, CA: Newcastle Publishing Company, 1972.

May, Edwin C., Victor Rubel, Joseph W. McMoneagle, and Loyd Auerbach. *ESP Wars: East and West.* Palo Alto, CA: Laboratories for Fundamental Research, 2014. Reprinted with Crossroads Press, 2016.

Mitchell, Edgar D. *Psychic Exploration: A Challenge for Science.* Edited by John White. New York: G. P. Putnam's Sons, 1974.

Priestly, J. B. *Man and Time.* New York: Crescent Books, 1989.

Rhine, Louisa E. *ESP in Life and Lab: Tracing Hidden Channels.* New York: Macmillan, 1967.

———. *The Invisible Picture.* Jefferson, NC: McFarland & Company, 1981.

Rogo, D. Scott, ed. *Mind Beyond the Body.* New York: Penguin, 1978.

———. *The Poltergeist Experience.* New York: Penguin, 1979.

Roll, William G. *The Poltergeist.* 2d ed. Metuchen, NJ: Scarecrow Press, 1976.

Rose, Ronald. *Living Magic.* New York: Rand McNally, 1956.

Stevenson, Ian. *Cases of the Reincarnation Type: Ten Cases in India. Vol. 1.* Charlottesville, VA: University Press of Virginia, 1975.

————. *Cases of the Reincarnation Type: Ten Cases in Sri Lanka. Vol. 2.* Charlottesville, VA: University Press of Virginia, 1977.

————. *Cases of the Reincarnation Type: Twelve Cases in Lebanon and Turkey. Vol. 3.* Charlottesville, VA: University Press of Virginia, 1980.

————. *Cases of the Reincarnation Type: Twelve Cases in Thailand and Burma. Vol. 4.* Charlottesville, VA: University Press of Virginia, 1983

————. *Twenty Cases Suggestive of Reincarnation.* 2d rev. ed. Charlottesville, VA: University Press of Virginia, 1974.

Ullman, Montague, and Nan Zimmerman. *Working with Dreams.* Los Angeles: Jeremy P. Tarcher, 1979.

Ullman, Montague, Stanley Krippner, and Alan Vaughan. *Dream Telepathy.* 2d ed. Jefferson, NC: McFarland & Company, 1989.

Van de Castle, Robert. *Our Dreaming Minds: The History and Psychology of Dreaming.* Virginia Beach, VA: Inner Vision Publishing, 1988.

Organizations of Note to Contact for Further Information

International Association for the Study of Dreams:
  www.asdreams.org

Parapsychological Association: www.parapsych.org

Rhine Research Center: www.rhine.org

Rhine Education Center: www.rhineeducationcenter.org

Parapsychology Foundation: www.parapsychology.org

International Association for Near Death Studies:
  www.iands.org

Institute of Noetic Studies: www.noetic.org

Forever Family Foundation: www.foreverfamilyfoundation.org

GET MORE AT LLEWELLYN.COM

Visit us online to browse hundreds of our books and decks, plus sign up to receive our e-newsletters and exclusive online offers.

- • Free tarot readings • Spell-a-Day • Moon phases
- • Recipes, spells, and tips • Blogs • Encyclopedia
- • Author interviews, articles, and upcoming events

GET SOCIAL WITH LLEWELLYN

Find us on

Facebook

www.Facebook.com/LlewellynBooks

Follow us on

www.Twitter.com/Llewellynbooks

GET BOOKS AT LLEWELLYN

LLEWELLYN ORDERING INFORMATION

Order online: Visit our website at www.llewellyn.com to select your books and place an order on our secure server.

Order by phone:
- • Call toll free within the U.S. at 1-877-NEW-WRLD (1-877-639-9753)
- • Call toll free within Canada at 1-866-NEW-WRLD (1-866-639-9753)
- • We accept VISA, MasterCard, American Express and Discover

Order by mail:
Send the full price of your order (MN residents add 6.875% sales tax) in U.S. funds, plus postage and handling to: Llewellyn Worldwide, 2143 Wooddale Drive Woodbury, MN 55125-2989

POSTAGE AND HANDLING

STANDARD (U.S. & Canada):
(Please allow 12 business days)
$30.00 and under, add $4.00.
$30.01 and over, FREE SHIPPING.

INTERNATIONAL ORDERS:
$16.00 for one book, plus $3.00 for each additional book.

Visit us online for more shipping options.
Prices subject to change.

FREE CATALOG!

To order, call
1-877-
NEW-WRLD
ext. 8236
or visit our
website

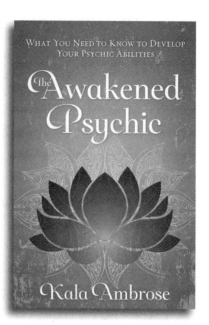

The Awakened Psychic
What You Need to Know to Develop Your Psychic Abilities
KALA AMBROSE

The Awakened Psychic is a guide to developing your inner psychic and tuning in to your intuitive wisdom. With hands-on exercises and stories from the author's practice, this book is all about lifting the veil between the worlds, seeing into the future, and connecting with spirits and loved ones on the other side. Join Kala Ambrose as she explores ideas and techniques for enhancing your psychic abilities and making the most of your intuitive talents, including:

- How to build a powerful energy field for psychic self-defense
- The difference between being psychic and being a medium
- Techniques to heighten your psychic abilities
- How ghosts and spirits are different
- How to awaken your powerful inner intuitive oracle
- The difference between an intuitive hunch and being psychic
- Techniques to connect with spirit guides and your higher self

Everyone has intuitive ability at some level, and those abilities can be helpful tools in making decisions, following your dreams, enhancing your relationships, and building a business or career that you enjoy. In this book, you'll discover the different kinds of psychic abilities and how they work together so that you can manifest your destiny and live a spiritually fulfilled life.

978-0-7387-4901-3, 216 pp., 5 ¼ x 8   **$15.99**

Dream
Interpretation

For Beginners

Understand the Wisdom of Your Sleeping Mind

DIANE BRANDON

Dream Interpretation for Beginners
Understand the Wisdom of Your Sleeping Mind
Diane Brandon

Decode the messages that your dreams may be trying to give you. Exploring your world of dreams, as well as your world of sleep, can enrich your life, improve your relationships, and help you achieve a sense of personal unfolding. *Dream Interpretation for Beginners* shows you how to use dreams for personal and spiritual growth, as well as improved problem-solving and deeper insight into your life.

978-0-7387-4191-8, 312 pp., 5 ³⁄₁₆ x 8　　　　　**$15.99**

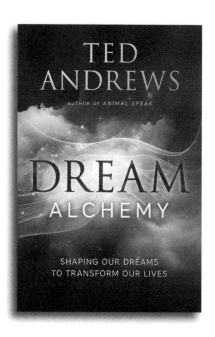

TED
ANDREWS
AUTHOR OF *ANIMAL SPEAK*

DREAM
ALCHEMY

SHAPING OUR DREAMS
TO TRANSFORM OUR LIVES

Dream Alchemy
Shaping Our Dreams to Transform Our Lives
TED ANDREWS

Back in print with a brand new cover for a new generation of dream explorers to enjoy, *Dream Alchemy* shows us how to gain control of dream states and use their transformative energies through safe and easy methods. Bestselling author Ted Andrews helps us stimulate greater dream activity, experience the power of lucid dreaming, discover controlled out-of-body experiences, awaken our inner selves, and much more.

Using dream totems and mandalas, exercises in metamorphosis, and ancient dream guardians, this guide to dream alchemy presents the process of becoming a shapeshifter—someone who can shift between the waking and dreaming worlds. When we control the dream state, we can unveil our inner potential, clear the debris from our subconscious, and be inspired to reshape our lives for a better future.

978-0-7387-4772-9, 264 pp., 6 x 9   **$15.99**

Dream Sight
A Dictionary and Guide for Interpreting Any Dream
Dr. Michael Lennox

Most dream dictionaries contain brief, overly generic meanings of the universal symbols that appear in our dreams. *Dream Sight* is different. With in-depth, classic meanings and an empowering technique for personalized interpretation, *Dream Sight* is the most complete and balanced guide to understanding your dreams.

Based on twenty years of experience, psychologist and renowned dream expert Dr. Michael Lennox presents his easy and practical three-step approach. Begin by reading the universal symbols in your dreams, then consider the context, and finally pinpoint your unique personal associations. This method leads to deeper, more profound interpretations that will unlock the mysteries of your unconscious mind. You'll also get insight into common types of dreams—recurring, precognitive, nightmares, and more—plus advice for remembering your dreams and looking at them objectively.

Combining warmth and a touch of irreverence, *Dream Sight* is both a unique teaching tool and a fun reference guide that gives you everything you need to understand your dreams and your innermost self.

Features an alphabetized list of over 300 dream symbols and images with classic meanings.

978-0-7387-2602-1, 408 pp., 6 x 9   **$19.95**

Lucid
Dreaming

For Beginners

Simple Techniques for Creating Interactive Dreams

MARK McELROY

Lucid Dreaming for Beginners
Simple Techniques for Creating Interactive Dreams
MARK MCELROY

In a lucid dream, you're aware that you're dreaming...so you can transform your dreams into fabulous adventures. From flying to traveling through time to visiting loved ones in spirit form, this book makes it easy for you to experience anything you wish.

Popular author Mark McElroy presents a simple and effective 90-day plan for achieving lucid dreams. Along with step-by-step instructions and practical tips, Mark shares entertaining and enlightening stories from other lucid dreamers. Once you've mastered self-awareness while sleeping, you can use lucid dreaming to:

- Live your fantasies
- Improve health and wellness
- Discover past lives
- Consult dream guides
- Enhance your spirituality
- Solve real-life problems
- Explore alternate realities

978-0-7387-0887-4, 288 pp., 5 ³⁄₁₆ x 8   **$14.95**

GRAHAM NICHOLLS

NAVIGATING

THE OUT-OF-BODY

EXPERIENCE

RADICAL
NEW
TECHNIQUES